MAKING THERAPY WORK

MAKING
THERAPY
WORK

◆

Your Guide to Choosing, Using, and Ending Therapy

FREDDA BRUCKNER-GORDON, D.S.W.

BARBARA KUERER GANGI, C.S.W.

GERALDINE URBACH WALLMAN, D.S.W.

1817

HARPER & ROW, PUBLISHERS, NEW YORK
CAMBRIDGE, PHILADELPHIA, SAN FRANCISCO
LONDON, MEXICO CITY, SÃO PAULO, SINGAPORE, SYDNEY

FIRST EDITION

Designed by Helen Barrow

To our families who provided the love and support we needed.

Robert and Emily
Rob, Jess, and Theo
Shelly and Josh

Contents

ACKNOWLEDGMENTS

This book has been evolving for the ten years that we have been meeting together to share our ideas about how to help our clients. We have each studied a number of theoretical approaches and employ a rich array of therapeutic strategies. While we have always had differences, we agree on a great deal about how to be helpful. Year by year and case by case we have noticed that our clients' success frequently does not depend on the severity of their problems but rather on their active involvement in their therapy. This book translates this lesson into a way of helping people make therapy work for them.

A great many people have had a part in the writing of this book. Those who tested the book in its drafts and contributed their ideas, support, and enthusiasm:

Our readers: Aline Couture, Elaine Everhart, Bette Fried, Barbara Green, David Glubo, Steve Karakashian, Renee Gail Kotler, Miriam Kuerer, Ilka Peck, Jerry Perlman, Lynn Schnurnberger, Gerda Schulman, Rachelle Smith, Michael Stallmeyer, Rose Gangi Stallmeyer, and Toni Swanson.

Our friends, colleagues, helpers, and mentors: Pam Atkins, Pat Belanoff, Martin S. Bergmann, Linda and Howard Bezoza, Janet Brazner, Anne Brooks, Robert Catenaccio, Carol Ann DiFiore, Alice Entin, Connie Fite, Zenia Fleigel, Elsa Goldstein, Lila King Hammer, Stuart Johnson, Ruth and Joseph Katz, Russ Karasik, Frank Kuerer, Elsa Leichter, Katherine Gordy Levine, Peggy Levine, Barry Marshall, Cynthia Merman, Barbara Pichler, Chaya Piotrkowski, Dominick Riccio, Dorothy Lander Rosen, Betsy Ross, Terry Simerly, Rickie Shuster, Larry Stallman, Bep Udink, Bill and Dorothy Urbach, Deborah Ward, Marian Weisberg, and Reed Whittle.

Carole Marshall, who helped shape the book in its beginnings. Frances Goldin, our agent, for seeing the possibilities in our project. Janet Goldstein, our editor at Harper & Row, for her knowledge, enthusiasm, and formidable patience. And most especially our clients who gave of their experiences and their wisdom so that we could pass it on to you.

Thank you all.

The first-person quotations in this book accurately reflect the feelings, experiences, and circumstances expressed by individuals engaged in the therapy process, but all names, locales, and identifying details have been changed.

A Guide to
Making Therapy Work

Psychotherapy may be the most important purchase in your life—not only because of the investment of money, time, and effort but because therapy offers the possibility of changing your life in a way that nothing else can.

However, too often people approach therapy with very little information and no real idea of how to make it work for them. Some may even avoid therapy because it seems mysterious, beyond their understanding or control.

Psychotherapy needn't be mysterious, and there are specific steps you can take to make your therapy rewarding. This book can help you get the most out of your therapy, just as your therapy can help you get the most out of your life. Owning this book can be like having a friend who is a therapist. You can refer to it with your questions and your worries. It has been designed to accompany you through your therapy, offering information, support, suggestions, and an opportunity to engage in a dialogue about a unique personal experience. We hope that you will approach this book in the same way that you will approach your psychotherapy—an an active participant.

The Rules for Success in Therapy represent the major themes that will be elaborated in this book. You will find practical suggestions about how to follow the rules to a successful outcome in your therapy.

Rules for Success in Therapy

- Choose your therapist carefully.
- Make yourself an active partner with your therapist.
- Do what you can to deepen the relationship with your therapist.
- Formulate therapy goals and keep your attention on your progress.
- Use everything that happens to learn and grow.

- Try out what you are learning both in and out of your therapy.
- Take the time you need to leave thoughtfully.

How to Use This Book

There is no one right way to use this book. You can read it from cover to cover or use it as a reference when you discover an interest or a need. There is a series of tasks, explanations, client quotations, and thought-provoking exercises to reassure, stimulate, and inform you. This book is meant to be read and reread, written in, and kept as private as you wish. Some sections will take more time and some less time; feel free to go at your own pace.

◆ **About the tasks.**   The book will take you through the beginning, middle, and ending phases of therapy by presenting a progression of tasks for you to undertake in each part of the process. It will inform you about what you can expect in each phase of therapy and suggest what you can do to improve your chances for success. The tasks are designed to increase your awareness, help you to stay active, and move you on to the next phase of your therapy.

◆ **About the exercises.**   This book is a workbook, and you will be encouraged to participate actively by responding to checklists and to questions that may disturb and enlighten you. As in therapy, your involvement with this book will make it most likely that you get what you hoped for.

There is space for your responses on the pages of the book, and you may want to read with a pen or pencil in hand to capture your spontaneous reactions. If you find you want to say more than the space permits, begin a separate diary as a companion to the book. You can use the diary to respond to material in the book or to record your thoughts, feelings, experiences, dreams, and fantasies. You may enjoy reviewing what you have written from time to time, to see how you are progressing.

◆ **About the quotations.**   Throughout the book, you will find quotations about the experience of being in therapy. They are included to help you understand the text and to engage as fully as possible in the exercises. Many of us are encouraged to hear about how others have worked to overcome difficulties and have enriched their lives in therapy.

How to Get What You Want from This Book

The use you will make of this book will depend on who you are and where you are in your therapy. Some of the readers who will find this book helpful are:

• ***Those considering therapy.*** Trying to describe psychotherapy in words is a bit like trying to describe dance to a blind person; words can tell only part of the story. The participatory nature of this book will help you to get a feel for what therapy can be like. The quotations can give you an idea about who can make use of therapy and what kinds of problems can be addressed. You will also find references in the Resources section to fictional and nonfictional accounts of therapy that can add to your understanding.

• ***Clients just beginning therapy.*** The next several chapters will lead you through the process of choosing and beginning therapy. In Chapter 1, you will find help in thinking about yourself and your life and describing where you are and where you want to be. Chapter 2 will guide you to an appropriate decision about whether to try therapy.

You will want to make a thoughtful choice of therapist. Chapter 3 informs you on the various kinds of therapy that are available, and Chapter 4 provides practical advice in choosing the right therapist for you. The Resource section contains names of organizations that can help you in your search.

Chapter 5 provides suggestions for making the most of the beginning phase of your therapy.

• ***Clients in the middle of therapy.*** Chapters 6 through 8 will help you use everything that happens in your life to learn and grow. You can learn what you can do to deepen the working relationship with your therapist, what you can do to get through the inevitable hard times, and how to integrate what you are learning in therapy into your life. Once you begin to use the therapy tools for yourself, you are on your way to becoming your own therapist.

• *Clients who want to evaluate their therapy.* Most clients have doubts from time to time, and it can be reassuring to know that you can evaluate your therapy at any point. Chapter 9 leads you through a thorough evaluation. If you find that indeed there is a problem that you and your therapist cannot resolve, you will learn how and when to seek a consultation and when it makes sense to change therapists.

• *Clients deciding to end their therapy.* You can find help in deciding when to end your therapy in Chapter 10 and a step-by-step guide to the ending process in Chapter 11.

• *Clients returning to therapy.* Before you return to therapy, read through this book, especially Chapter 9, to sort out what worked and what didn't work in your prior therapy. Chapter 3 will help you think about whether to return to your previous therapist or start with someone new. If you decide to see a different therapist, Chapters 3 and 4 will guide you to the right therapy and therapist for you.

• *Those concerned about someone else.* It can be very difficult to see someone you care about in pain. The Appendix provides information about the tricky business of deciding when a child or parent may need therapy and how and when to approach a friend, family member, or colleague about his or her difficulties. The Resources section suggests books about the specific problems that concern you and organizations that can be contacted for assistance.

• *Practicing psychotherapists.* If you are a new therapist, you can learn your part in guiding your clients through the beginning, middle, and ending phases of therapy. Reading about the experiences of many clients in different stages and various kinds of therapy can extend your own experience as a therapist.

Psychotherapy is an exciting journey of self-discovery and change. Bon voyage.

•1•
Taking Stock

We all long for rich, rewarding lives—satisfying work, caring relationships, and good feelings about ourselves. Yet at times we may find that we have lost our way. Along with our efforts to grow and make our lives better, there can be a countervailing force that keeps old, self-defeating patterns in place. During such periods we may begin to wonder what, if anything, can help.

For many of us, therapy holds the answer. If you are going through a particularly bad time right now or have a pervasive sense of dissatisfaction with your life, you may be considering psychotherapy. The following two chapters are designed to guide you in making that choice, first by giving you an organized way to think about yourself and your life, then by sorting through your reasons for considering therapy, and finally by exploring and helping you to overcome any reservations you may have about therapy.

This chapter will help you to take stock of yourself, to sum up where you are and where you would like to be. You can use what you discover to help you decide if you want to begin therapy, to guide you to an appropriate therapist, and to prepare for your initial consultation. Later you can use this chapter as a written record to check your progress and to decide when you have gotten what you wanted from therapy.

This chapter can seem daunting, especially if you feel a sense of urgency about getting help. You may want to take stock of yourself and your life gradually over time or return to this chapter when you are feeling more settled.

◆ Task 1 ◆
Think About Yourself

Our sense of ourselves is complex and not always easy to capture in words. The next series of exercises will help you explore different aspects of your experience: your relationships, your self-esteem, your feelings, and your ability to take care of yourself and to think clearly. You will consider not only what is troubling you but also what feels good about your life. You will see where you are thriving and where you could grow. At the same time you may begin to see yourself slightly differently, as you might if you were actually in therapy.

Relationships

Having satisfying relationships brings a sense of belonging and contentment to our lives. Sometimes relationships fall into unsatisfying patterns, causing us unhappiness or pain. The quality of our relationships is an important part of how we see ourselves. Check any of the statements below that apply to you.

I am satisfied with my relationships with
_____ my friends.
_____ my parents.
_____ my siblings, their mates, and children.
_____ my boss.
_____ my teachers.
_____ my co-workers.
_____ I have at least one friend who really knows me.
_____ I am sure that I will have a partner with whom to share my life.
_____ I have a close and satisfying love relationship.
_____ I have a number of people in my life whom I trust.
_____ I have lasting friendships.
_____ I can end relationships that are not good for me.
_____ or, _____

Complete the following sentences.

What I like about my relationships is

I am unhappy about my relationships because

◆

"I have good friends, but somehow that doesn't mean much. What I really want is a man to share my life."

"I don't get along with my daughter. I love her, sure, but she makes me so angry that I seem to hate her too. I feel more and more like a bad mother."

"My career is a mess, but I've discovered that I have a few good friends who stand by me no matter what."

◆

Feelings

Emotions enrich us and add complexity and depth to our lives. Sometimes we may find our emotions too painful and difficult to manage. Although experiencing sadness, anger, jealousy, and fear is a part of being human, at times these feelings may be overwhelming or too difficult to explain.

We may worry because we do not experience a full range of emotions; we feel numb when others feel joy or sadness, pleasure or anger. We may even cut off our feelings or act impetuously when we experience strong emotions.

While feelings may appear to arise mysteriously, it is possible to understand their source. The more you understand what you feel, the more you can accept your feelings and manage them constructively. See what you can learn by completing the following statements.

I feel sad about

I feel guilty about

I feel anxious when

I feel angry about

I feel jealous of

I feel happy about

Most of the time I feel

I am overwhelmed by feelings of

It is difficult for me to feel

How optimistic are you that things will turn out well for you? Optimism creates reinforcing cycles. Optimism brings positive responses from others; this feedback increases our good feelings about ourselves and our projects; and in turn our increased optimism leads to even more positive feedback. Most important, optimism encourages us to be active and take risks, which makes positive outcomes more likely.

I feel hopeful when

I feel hopeless when

Not only are feelings a meaningful part of our internal selves, how and when we express and act on our feelings can make an important difference in our external lives.

If I could change anything about the way I express or manage my feelings, it would be

◆

"I have no idea what is going on. I'm edgy, everything gets to me. I cry at the drop of a hat. I have this vague feeling that something awful is going to happen."

"When I was a kid, my parents called me Sarah Bernhardt because I was so dramatic. As a grown-up, I have found that other people actually appreciate me for being expressive."

"I drag myself out of bed every morning, can barely stay awake, and can't wait to get home at night. Then I sit in front of the tube, like a zombie."

◆

Taking Care of Yourself

All of us want to be competent and in charge of our lives. We want to function well in our everyday life, keeping up with our work, being responsible to others where we need to be, while taking good care of ourselves. Some of our behavior may be either self-defeating or troublesome, and we wonder how to change.

Check the statements below that apply to you.

_____ I am satisfied with the way I perform at work or school.
_____ I complete my work without procrastinating or overworking.
_____ I have an organized and comfortable place to live.
_____ I am responsible in the way I handle money.
_____ I am satisfied with my drinking, smoking, and eating habits.
_____ I go after what I want.
_____ I achieve most of my goals.
_____ I am dependable with my family and friends.
_____ I have a satisfying balance between work and play.
_____ I'm comfortable with my sex life.
_____ I get enough exercise.
_____ I avoid self-defeating behavior.
_____ or, _____

◆

"When I first entered therapy I could spend money without thinking and never had enough. It took a while to learn that I couldn't hold on to my money because I felt guilty about having so much more than my brothers. I haven't worked it all out yet, but I have noticed that I am more careful about what I do with my money."

"Food seems to control me. I don't eat because I'm hungry; I eat, get numb, and feel awful."

"Every time I go to my parents' house I get into an argument with my father. I lose it when I'm around him."

◆

Thinking

Being able to think clearly allows us to evaluate reality accurately and to plan appropriate responses. Our ability to think can be compromised by stress, by intense feelings, or by misconceptions and prejudices. Some of us have simply never learned how to think about our internal world or about events outside ourselves.

Check any of the following statements that apply to you.

_____ People usually understand what I say.
_____ I avoid difficult subjects by not thinking about them.
_____ I have common sense.
_____ I can make decisions without too much difficulty.
_____ I seem to be in a fog a lot of the time.
_____ I can have strong feelings and continue to think clearly.
_____ I'm stuck thinking about the same thing over and over again.
_____ I can think through my problems.
_____ I'm afraid I am going crazy.
_____ I am confused.
_____ or, _____

◆

"It's impossible to concentrate lately. I get distracted at work and at school. My thoughts race off in all directions."

"I try but I can't stop thinking about him. I hardly know him, and he occupies my thoughts night and day."

◆

Self-esteem

Self-esteem is the core of thoughts and feelings about ourselves that we carry with us through rewarding and frustrating experiences. With positive self-esteem, our sense of self is constant; it doesn't depend on the situation: Even when trouble occurs, we can maintain confidence that we are basically worthwhile and lovable.

Check any of the following statements that apply to you.

_____ I am smart enough.
_____ I deserve good things in life.
_____ I can make mistakes without feeling bad about myself.
_____ I am satisfied with my appearance.
_____ I am a good friend.
_____ I usually do things well.
_____ I am lovable.
_____ I usually live up to my expectations of myself.

Complete the following statements.

I wish I were more

I wish I were less

What I like best about myself

◆

"My husband says that I don't really see myself when I look in the mirror. No matter how much weight I lose, I feel fat and ugly."

"I think that I am addicted to sex. I need that constant validation to feel that I am alive."

"I want to be special. I don't think that I could like myself very much if I settled for being ordinary."

"Not much has turned out the way I thought it would in my life, but over all I guess I am at peace with who and what I am."

◆ Task 2 ◆
Think About Your Life

We all face challenging and difficult experiences as well as sustaining and nurturing ones. Our lives differ in the number and kinds of challenges we have to face, the resources we have to manage them, and how available our environment is to support and sustain us.

Taking a look at your childhood experiences can help you get some perspective on the events and circumstances that shaped your life today.

Early Experiences

Certain experiences seem to have a particularly significant impact on children and may continue to influence adult life. What do you remember about your childhood? To help you recall important early experiences, respond to the next exercise with whatever comes to mind.

These childhood and family experiences were important to me

The statements below describe dramatic situations that almost always have impact on our adult lives. Check those that apply to you, and add any other positive or painful circumstances that may have influenced your life in the space at the end of each list.

As a child, I
_____ was uprooted many times by family moves.
_____ grew up in a country at war.
_____ was placed in a foster home.
_____ had a learning disability
_____ was handicapped/seriously ill.
_____ was sexually molested.
_____ was less attractive than my peers.
_____ did poorly in school.
_____ was lonely.
_____ suffered the effects of racial, economic, or sexual prejudice.
_____ was unpopular.
_____ had a sick/handicapped brother or sister.
_____ was adopted.
_____ had a brother or sister who died.
_____ witnessed violence.
_____ was very poor.
_____ or, _____

My parent(s)
_____ was an alcoholic.
_____ abused drugs.
_____ was hospitalized for a mental illness.
_____ abandoned me when I was young.
_____ survived the Holocaust.
_____ was physically abusive.
_____ divorced.
_____ was famous.
_____ was in trouble with the law.
_____ was handicapped or frequently ill.
_____ died.
_____ committed suicide.
_____ or, _____

Complete the following statements.

The childhood experience(s) that most burdened my adult life

The childhood experience(s) that most enriched my adult life

◆

"I was brought up poor and went to a junior college. Now I want to be with middle-class professional people, but I'm tongue-tied. I don't fit in with my family and I don't fit in with educated people either."

"There were no tragedies or traumas in my life, but it was miserable nonetheless. I felt alone, unloved, and lacking direction."

"I was born during the Second World War and my dad was gone and my mom had a lot to manage. I often wonder what my life would have been like if she'd had more time and energy for me."

"I grew up without a lot of the nice things that my friends had, and I struggled to get my education. I may be fooling myself, but when I compare how I turned out with how some of those more privileged kids messed up their lives, I think maybe I was lucky. I learned to go after what I wanted and to work hard."

◆

Coping

Stress has an enormous effect on how we feel and how well we do. An inevitable part of life, stress comes with positive change as well as with difficult circumstances. A manageable amount of stress can be energizing, while too much can be debilitating. The amount of stress that we experience doesn't just depend upon the events; our ability to cope varies from time to time. Take the time to think of the events that are shaping your life currently. The following events are almost always stressful; you may realize that other, less intense experiences have been stressful for you. Be sure to add any instances of stress you've experienced to this list.

In the past year I have experienced
_____ the death of a (spouse) (family member) (friend).
_____ (the loss of a job) (the search for a new job) (a change in jobs) (promotion) (retirement).
_____ prejudice or limitations imposed on me because of my (race) (religion) (sex) (sexual orientation) (age) (physical handicap).
_____ (serious illness) (injury).
_____ (marriage) (divorce) (separation) (reconciliation).
_____ (moving) (searching for a new home) (buying or selling my home).
_____ (pregnancy) (the birth of a child).
_____ beginning or ending school.
_____ discord with (family) (friends) (neighbors) (boss) (co-workers).
_____ a child leaving home.
_____ serious difficulties with a child.
_____ or, _____

How have you been affected by and managed this stress?

◆

"I can't pull myself together since my husband died. It's been eighteen months and I still can't stop crying."

"After years of fighting to get into management, I just got laid off. I feel bitter. Blacks still are the last hired and the first fired."

◆

Goals for the Future

Many of us have hopes and dreams for the future, dreams that begin in youth and continue throughout a lifetime. As children, we picture the kind of life we want, our occupation, our future life partner. Over time, we may realize some of our early goals and revise others in the face of the realities of grownup life. Goal setting can be a lifelong process that helps us to have a sense of direction and accomplishment.

We may not be inclined to think about the future. We may have learned that it is safer to take each day as it comes or we doubt that we can depend on anything good happening. It may seem boring or unnecessary to plan ahead. Yet it can be rewarding to consider the possibilities that goal setting can offer.

The following exercises will help you articulate your goals for the future. If you do begin psychotherapy, you can refer back to this section for guidance from time to time. Knowing what you want for yourself can help you decide what kind of therapist to look for, determine your goals for therapy, help you evaluate your therapy, and decide when your goals have been reached.

Imagine that it is two years from now and you have succeeded in changing some significant things about yourself or your circumstances. What is different and how are you affected?

Try the following exercise to set priorities for the changes you want to make. Complete the following statements.

I must do something about

It would make a positive change in my life if I would

It would be a good idea if I could do something about

◆

"All I've ever wanted to do was be a doctor. Now it looks like I won't be accepted into medical school. I've lost my whole sense of direction."

◆ Task 3 ◆
Sum Up Where You Are
and Where You'd Like to Be

Taking stock has given you a taste of the self-examination that psychotherapy encourages. One important ingredient has been present: your active involvement in looking at yourself. Some critical ingredients are missing: the collaboration between you and a therapist and the objectivity that another person can provide. The next exercise can bring you close to this kind of objectivity.

Pretend that you've stepped outside yourself. Take some time to look at yourself as you would look at a friend. Regarding that friend (yourself) benevolently, complete the exercise.

What I really like about _____ (insert your name) **is**

I wish he or she would do something about (describe the specific changes desired)

How do your friends and family think that you are doing? Are they pleased with you and how your life is going? Sometimes we think that we are okay, yet someone close to us is worried about us or dissatisfied with some aspect of our life.

It's not easy to evaluate feedback from friends and family. Sometimes we get contradictory messages: Our lover may appreciate our liveliness, while our mother is embarrassed by it. Yet we can learn something valuable about ourselves as we try to understand others' points of view. Return to the previous exercise and complete the statements from the viewpoint of someone who is concerned about you.

What do you think now that you have imagined how other people think about you and your life? You may want to reread what you have written in the chapter so far and think about your relationships with people, your emotional state, your self-esteem, and your ability to think clearly and take care of yourself.

I want to feel better about

I want to begin to

I want to stop

I am satisfied with

I would like to change

•2•
Choosing Therapy

TASKS

1. Learn When to Choose Therapy
2. Identify and Work with Your Reservations About Therapy
3. Make Your Choice

Psychotherapy can help us improve our relationships, be more in control of our lives and behavior, and generally feel better. It can help us clarify our thinking, achieve our life goals, improve our self-esteem, and increase our sense of hopefulness. It can help with specific problems or with more pervasive changes. It can help during a crisis or get us through a transition from one life stage to another. We can come and go over the years as needed or stay until we feel well equipped to live a rich, productive life.

◆ Task 1 ◆
Learn When to Choose Therapy

Just as certain physical symptoms and illnesses require the attention of a physician, certain emotional symptoms require the immediate attention of a psychotherapist. (See the adjacent box.) But your situation does not have to be desperate for you to choose therapy. Being dissatisfied with some part of your life, feeling distressed, or needing help to cope with a problem is enough reason to begin psychotherapy.

EMERGENCY SYMPTOM CHECKLIST

Check the statements below that are true for you. (If you have a friend or relative suffering from any of these symptoms, refer to the Appendix: "When Someone You Care About Needs Help.")

_____ I frequently find myself in dangerous situations.

_____ I think about hurting myself or others.

_____ I have made a suicide attempt.

_____ I am considered underweight and continue to diet.

_____ I am extremely depressed.

_____ I can't sleep.

_____ I worry that someone wants to hurt me.

_____ It seems like I am going crazy.

_____ I have uncontrollable crying spells.

_____ I am panicked most of the time.

_____ I am abusing alcohol and/or drugs.

_____ I cannot take care of myself or do any of my work.

_____ I have been seeing or hearing things that aren't there.

_____ I can't control my thoughts.

_____ I have physically hurt myself or someone else.

If you checked one or more of the statements, find a therapist immediately. Untreated, these symptoms can be dangerous! Fast, efficient help is available. You can turn to "Where to Find Help in an Emergency" on page 57 to find specialized help for these symptoms.

Some symptoms require a consultation with a physician: any loss of consciousness, or decreased attention span, short-term memory, or an inability to accomplish structured tasks.

Often, dependence on chemicals like alcohol and drugs responds better to psychotherapy combined with alcohol or drug treatment programs like Alcoholics Anonymous. See "Resources," page 239, for information about programs for chemical dependency.

Here are examples of why some people seek therapy. Check those that apply to you.

_____ I want more out of my life.
_____ I am preoccupied with a problem.
_____ I feel unhappy most of the time.
_____ I am overwhelmed by my problems.
_____ I can't seem to control my behavior.
_____ Someone I care about wants me to go to therapy.
_____ I am anxious or depressed.
_____ I don't really like myself.
_____ I do things that are self-destructive.
_____ I am not doing as well as I'd like to at work or school.
_____ I want to have a love relationship.
_____ I don't get along well with my parents or children.
_____ I feel hopeless.
_____ I don't fit in anywhere.
_____ My life has no direction.
_____ I want to learn more about myself or understand myself better.
_____ or, _____

◆

"I am tired of half living, tired of being tired all the time."

"My best friend just got married. I'm so jealous of her that I can't be happy for her. I don't want to end up bitter and alone."

"It looks like we are not going to be able to have a baby of our own, and suddenly everything tastes like ashes to me."

◆

Even if you are uncertain about your reasons, wanting to be in therapy is enough of a signal to schedule a consultation with a therapist. A consulting psychotherapist will help you clarify your reasons for seeking therapy.

◆ Task 2 ◆
Identify and Work with
Your Reservations About Therapy

Often people have fears about therapy. You may have heard things about therapy that make it seem like a difficult undertaking. Here are some common reservations that beginning therapy clients have voiced. Check those that are familiar to you.

_____ Only weak people need help.
_____ I will become too dependent on my therapist.
_____ I'm afraid that if I start therapy I'll never leave.
_____ Therapy just helps people adjust to an unjust world.
_____ If I don't do it myself it doesn't count.
_____ Therapy doesn't really do any good anyway.
_____ I'll have to talk about all my personal issues with a stranger.
_____ Therapy will make me worse.
_____ I'll discover some deep horrible thing about myself.
_____ If I talk about things I'll only get more upset.
_____ Nobody can really help me.
_____ My therapist will be able to read my mind.
_____ Only crazy people need therapy.
_____ I just want to fix things up now, not rehash my whole life.
_____ I will find out that I'm going crazy.
_____ My family/spouse will think all our problems are my fault.
_____ People in therapy end up blaming their parents for everything.
_____ Therapy will make me a boring person.
_____ Therapy will cost a fortune.
_____ or, _____

Sorting through your reservations can make it possible to move on in spite of them. Your fears can become less fierce and paralyzing once they are out in the open.

Here are some practical suggestions about what you can do to deal with your reservations about therapy:

- *Talk to someone you trust about your fears.* This can help, particularly if that person has been in therapy or is knowledgeable about therapy. Getting support from someone can also help to counteract any isolation that may be developing while you are feeling bad.

- *Get more information about what happens in therapy.* Read the rest of this book and turn to "Resources" for suggestions.
- *Have a consultation with a therapist and discuss your reservations.* Since many clients have similar concerns on beginning therapy, most therapists will be prepared to talk with you about your doubts.
- *Begin therapy with an agreement to work for a few sessions.* This way you can check out what the actual experience is like for you. At the end of that time you can decide whether to continue.

♦ Task 3 ♦
Make Your Choice

Remember that fears about therapy are natural, and they do not have to be put to rest before you begin. The next two chapters are designed to help you make a careful, informed choice of therapist. Even after you have started, you can continue to evaluate how helpful therapy is for you. Try to weigh the potential benefits against the potential difficulties by answering the following questions.

What is the worst thing that can happen to me if I begin therapy?

What is the best thing that can happen to me if I begin therapy?

The idea of courage applauds people who embark on an adventure despite their fear. The rest of this book will help you to make your experience in therapy positive and productive.

·3·

Thinking About Your Future Therapy

TASKS

---

1. Imagine Your Ideal Therapist and Therapy Situation
2. Learn About Therapeutic Strategies
3. Learn About the Schools of Psychotherapy
4. Learn About Couple, Group, and Family Therapy
5. Decide What You Will Look For

Now that you have decided to try psychotherapy, your next step is to learn about the kinds of therapists and therapies available. Before making the first phone call, you need to do some thinking about your unique requirements. The therapist you decide to see must be right for you, someone you can trust with your deepest feelings and the most private areas of your life, someone who you believe can help solve problems you have been unable to solve yourself, someone with whom you can develop rapport.

The guidelines in this chapter will help you think through your preferences so that you will be in a good position to search for a suitable and compatible therapist. With some persistence, patience, and self-reflection, you can figure out what you want in a therapist.

Therapies differ in important ways. In this chapter, you will find descriptions of the most common schools of therapy, along with exercises to help you choose the one that is most congruent with your needs. You don't want to go to the butcher shop for flowers.

Note: Since this chapter and the next contain a great deal of information, you may want to read those sections that most relate to what interests you right now. The following list can help you find what you need:

- If you need help immediately, turn to page 57.
- If you want to learn more about different kinds of therapy, turn to page 41.
- If you are wondering whether to return to your former therapist, turn to page 59.
- If you are wondering whether you need group, couple, or family therapy, turn to page 49.
- If you think you need a therapist with special training, turn to page 33.
- If you have questions about tranquilizers and antidepressants, turn to page 33.
- If you are wondering what to expect in a clinic, turn to page 66.
- If you want to know about costs and other practical considerations, turn to page 62.
- If you are wondering how to prepare for an initial interview, turn to page 65.
- If you are wondering how to evaluate whether you can work successfully with a particular therapist, turn to page 67.

Even if you decide to read only certain sections, do complete the first task.

◆ Task 1 ◆
Imagine Your Ideal Therapist and Therapy Situation

You may have been in therapy before and have definite ideas about what you are looking for this time. Or you may be so new at this that you are overwhelmed and have no idea what is available, let alone what you want.

Even if you've never had direct experience with psychotherapy, your friends may have told you about their therapy and the media have introduced you to different therapists. You may have been put off by, or intrigued by, or indifferent to what you've heard. Your reactions can give you some clues about what you prefer.

Imagining your ideal therapist can help you define your expectations. Finding someone who matches your expectations in important ways can smooth your entry into therapy.

My ideal therapist is (check all those that apply and star any that are especially important to you).

_____ male	_____ sympathetic	_____ attractive
_____ female	_____ scholarly	_____ a social peer
_____ maternal/paternal	_____ warm	_____ tough
_____ practical	_____ objective	_____ accepting
_____ caring	_____ self-revealing	_____ wise
_____ stimulating	_____ soothing	_____ funny
_____ smart	_____ younger	_____ older
_____ authoritative	_____ perceptive	_____ gentle
_____ informal	_____ talkative	_____ flexible
_____ understanding	_____ formal	_____ direct
_____ consistent	_____ unafraid	_____ honest
_____ serious	_____ astute	_____ businesslike
_____ creative	_____ generous	_____ organized

These characteristics are important to me because

If you have been in therapy before, answer the following:

The qualities of my previous therapist(s) that I would like to find in my future therapist are

The qualities of my previous therapist(s) that I would like to avoid in my future therapist are

◆

"I want to see a man who is very bright, old, and wise, with a lot of credentials and experience."

"I need someone tough this time, someone who won't let me get away with things. I was in therapy before and I blabbered away and so did my psychiatrist. It was like we had an agreement to avoid painful subjects."

". . . nurturing without rescuing, enlightening without preaching, caring without controlling."

"My father is critical, distant. Any therapist I see has to be accepting."

"I want a therapist who listens well, doesn't make me feel as if my story has to be spicy, asks questions and gives opinions, lets some of her own personality show, and expresses warmth and concern where appropriate."

◆

Background

It may be very important to you to find a therapist who has had a particular experience or shares some of your background. For example, if your religion is very important to you, if you are a member of a minority group, or if you are struggling with how to parent your child, you may want to choose a therapist who shares these experiences. See page 97 about asking therapists personal questions.

It is important for my therapist to share or be knowledgeable about these particular aspects of my experience

◆

"How could I talk about my deepest feelings to a girl with no gray hair and no children of her own?"

"My therapist was just the kind of cheerleader type I would have hated and envied as a kid. The fact that we talked about my feelings and that she was so accepting helped me to accept myself more."

"There is no way that I'm going to talk about my sex life to a straight therapist."

"My therapist said that the sex of the therapist doesn't matter because, thanks to the phenomenon of transference, I would be able to experience her as though she were a man or a woman. It was amazing: she was right. She was my mother, father, and brother at different times."

"It has been important to have a therapist who knows first-hand what it is like to be a parent and didn't just learn about it from a book."

◆

Experience

It is commonly thought that therapists with a great deal of experience have more to offer their clients. At the same time, especially with very difficult situations, inexperienced therapists can often make up in optimism and enthusiasm what they lack in experience.

Training

Many people are confused about the various titles used by therapists. As you will understand from the descriptions below, these titles refer to academic and clinical training and to organizational affiliations.

Psychotherapists. The broadest and most inclusive term used to describe a therapist has no legal definition: states usually license or certify psychotherapists according to their various academic degrees. Each psychotherapist usually has two titles: psychotherapist and psychiatrist (M.D.); psychotherapist and social worker (M.S.W., D.S.W., or Ph.D.); psychotherapist and psychologist (Ph.D., Ed.D., or M.A.); psychotherapist and nurse (R.N. or M.A.); psychotherapist and pastoral counselor (M.A., M.Div., D.Div., D.Min., Ph.D.). In addition to their academic degrees, many of these professionals go on to study a specific theoretical approach to psychotherapy at a postgraduate institute.

Some psychotherapists have entered the profession from nonacademic routes and do not have these more "traditional" degrees. They may have studied with a mentor or at a training institute that does not offer an academic degree. Although some very talented therapists have been trained in this way, it is useful to ask for information about a therapist's credentials to assure yourself that he or she is well qualified.

Although there is no evidence that any one of the following academic disciplines has produced more qualified or successful therapists, you may find that your medical insurance covers only some of these disciplines. See "Resources," page 229, for information about professional organizations.

Clinical psychologists usually have a doctorate in clinical psychology (Ph.D.), although some states license psychologists with a doctorate in education (Ed.D.), a master's degree (M.A.), or a doctorate in psychotherapy (Psy.D.). Psychologists are specially trained to perform a variety of intelligence, personality, and other diagnostic tests. Other psychotherapists may refer their clients to psychologists if testing is deemed useful. Psychologists must be licensed by the state; in addition, they may be certified by the American Board of Examiners in Professional Psychology.

Clinical social workers earn a master's degree (M.S.W.) or a doctorate (D.S.W. or Ph.D.) in social work. The course of study emphasizes working directly with people to relieve their psychological or social distress. Although many social workers have private practices, most work in family agencies, hospitals, mental health, and child guidance clinics. More psychotherapists have academic training in social work than in any other discipline. Many states have licensing or certification procedures for social workers; and they may have been awarded the title "Board Certified Diplomate in Clinical Social Work" by the American Board of Examiners in Clinical Social Work.

Counselors have a master's degree, usually from a school of education. Often, counselors have expertise in working with school problems, rehabilitation, and employment problems. While most counselors are found in educational settings, increasing numbers are located in mental health agencies, private practice, and business settings. Professional counselors may be licensed or certified in the state in which they work and by the National Board for Certified Counselors of the National Academy of Certified Mental Health Counselors.

Marital and family therapists (marriage counselors) have an M.A., M.D., or M.S.W., a D.S.W., a Ph.D., or an Ed.D., and training specifically in marital and family therapy. A number of states have licensing for these professionals, who may also be clinical members of the American Association for Marriage and Family Therapy or the American Family Therapy Association.

Pastoral counselors are laymen or members of the clergy who are formally endorsed by their own religious denomination. In addition to theology, pastoral counselors have specialized training in counseling (an M.A., M.Div., D.Min., Ph.D., D.Div.).

Psychiatric nurses (R.N.), increasingly found in private practice, are registered nurses who have earned a master's degree and who usually practice in hospitals and community mental health centers. The American Nurses Association has a certification program for specialists in mental health nursing. Registered nurses are licensed by each state.

Psychiatrists are medical doctors (M.D.) who specialize in the field of diagnosing and treating people with emotional disturbances. They are the only mental health professionals who are trained to differentiate between the physical and emotional causes of emotional distress and to provide certain physical treatments such as medication and electroshock therapy. Most are affiliated with hospitals, where they can arrange for inpatient care when necessary. All psychiatrists are licensed by the state in which they practice; they may also be certified by the American Board of Psychiatry and Neurology.

Sex Therapists. In most states, anyone can call him/herself a sex therapist. Many sex therapists are psychotherapists with special training in sex therapy. There are, however, some who are trained only in sex therapy. Since the standards for this training can vary considerably, it is important to inquire about the kind of training a sex therapist has had and to favor a therapist who has achieved membership in the American Association of Sex Educators, Counselors and Therapists.

Psychoanalysts. With the exception of California, no state has a legal definition of a psychoanalyst. He or she may come from one of the traditional disciplines described above or from another field altogether. It is generally accepted that a psychoanalyst has studied psychoanalysis at a postgraduate institute of advanced study that offers a certificate but no academic degree. The student of psychoanalysis engages in a personal analysis while studying a particular analytic approach (see page 44 for some of them).

Special Expertise

A therapist may have expertise in one or more problem areas or work with a specific population. If you have a life-threatening problem like anorexia, violent or suicidal behavior, or alcohol or drug abuse, it is critical that you locate a therapist who has expertise in that area. Specialists in certain other problem areas, like phobias and sexual dysfunction, appear to have a better track record than nonspecialists. Many therapists have training or experience in working with specific problems like battered women, the handicapped, or Holocaust survivors and their children. Especially if you have been in therapy before and have found no relief for a particular problem, consider going to someone who is an authority on the subject. For more information, see "Resources," page 237.

◆

"It happened gradually. First my mother stopped shopping, then visiting us, and finally she wouldn't leave the house even to go to her own brother's funeral. The psychology clinic at the university began working with my mother's problem, agoraphobia. They started out by coming to the house and gradually worked her up to coming to them. They got her going again."

"I joined a group for adult children of alcoholics and found out that lots of us have trouble with asking for what we want and spend our time rescuing people we love."

◆

Tranquilizers and Antidepressants

Depending on the nature of your problem, medicine can help. While other physicians prescribe psychotropic medications, psychiatrists are best equipped to decide whether and what kind of medicine may be appropriate. Seeing a non-M.D. psychotherapist does not rule out the possibility of medication. A psychotherapist can refer you to an M.D. specialist who can evaluate how useful medication could be for you.

When it works, psychotropic medicine is very effective. It is not a panacea, however, and there are often side effects. A course of medication may be useful in addition to your psychotherapy. These are some of the symptoms medication has been known to help:

extreme anxiety	loss of interest in sex
hallucinations	loss of ability to perceive reality accurately
agitation	loss of energy
excessive sleeping	excessive energy
incapacitating depression	disordered thinking
delusions	panic
insomnia	phobias
early-morning wakening	psychosis
excessive tearfulness	

◆

"I used to think medication was a crutch. Well, crutches can be useful if you have a broken leg. The tranquilizer took enough of the edge off so I could think through my problems."

"I got more help with my depression from cognitive therapy than I did from medication."

"Years ago, my internist gave me a tranquilizer, and I kept refilling the prescription. The psychiatrist I went to, who is up-to-date on what medicine can do, told me I really needed an antidepressant. The right medication made all the difference."

◆

Some Options to Keep in Mind

Now it's time to consider your expectations of the therapy situation itself. Explore some of the possibilities in the exercise below.

The therapy that I want will focus on

_____ one specific problem *(issue oriented)*.

_____ increasing my self-awareness *(growth oriented)*.

_____ the here-and-now problems in my daily life.

_____ my inner life (my fantasies and dreams).

It will continue for

_____ a few weeks to a year *(short-term)*.

_____ two to three years.

_____ as long as necessary.

It will meet

_____ once a week.

_____ twice a week.

_____ three or more times a week.

_____ when I need it.

It will include
_____ my family.
_____ my partner.
_____ just me.
_____ other group members.

How would you describe your ideal therapy?

If you have been in therapy before, what would you like to be the same and what would you like to be different about your new therapy?

◆

"If I could get it, I would have therapy every day with a gentle, understanding therapist, who would comfort me."

"I would like to be in a very energetic, focused group where I would get some direction for my life."

"My first therapy helped me pick up the pieces after my marriage broke up. This time I want to be in an intensive therapy, go a couple of times a week for a few years, so that I can deal with the patterns that get me into miserable relationships with men."

"I don't want any big analysis, I want to find a therapist who will help us have enjoyable sex again."

◆ Task 2 ◆
Learn About Therapeutic Strategies

There is more than one way to do therapy. In fact, there are hundreds! How can you know which to choose?

Therapists use different strategies to help their clients.* In a perfect world, every therapist would employ a complete array of strategies and would vary them to match each client's needs. However, in the real world, few therapists are equally adept at or trained to use all the different strategies.

You may be in pain and feel you can tolerate only the most soothing and supportive therapy. At the other extreme, you may prefer to be challenged, feeling strong enough to handle an intense exploratory or confrontational approach. You may want a therapy that offers unique situations, exercises, or techniques for you to try out. Or you may prefer things to be as close as possible to what is familiar to you.

It is useful to learn about the strategies preferred by therapists trained in various schools of therapy, so that you can form some ideas about what might be helpful. The next set of exercises asks you to consider which therapeutic strategies you may want. Later you can choose a school of therapy that emphasizes the use of those strategies.

You may want to mark the most appealing strategies with a star, for convenient review.

SUPPORT

_____ **I want my therapist to be reassuring and encouraging, emphasizing my strengths and achievements.**

"He knew how hard it was for me to tell my parents that I am gay. He also knew how wrecked I was, keeping so much of my life a secret. He encouraged me to face them with who I really am and was confident that I could do it."

* The concept of therapeutic strategies and their descriptions are derived in part from the well developed scheme found in Frances, A., J. Clarkin, and S. Perry, *Differential Therapeutics in Psychiatry; The Art and Science of Treatment Selection.* New York: Brunner/Mazel, 1984. Also see Perry, S., A. Frances, and J. Clarkin, *A DSM-III Casebook of Differential Therapeutics: A Clinical Guide to Selection.* New York: Brunner/Mazel, 1985.

EDUCATION

_____ I want a therapist who will give information and teach me specific techniques to deal with my problems.

"Since I have learned what manic depression is and what my options are, I have stopped blaming myself and I understand how important it is to stay on my medication. I manage my life so much better now."

"Just learning what kind of behavior to expect in a four-year-old helped me to cope better as a father."

EXPLANATION OF WHY

_____ I want to understand why I behave, feel, and think the way I do.

"All I knew was that I was furious at her. When my therapist asked me why, I realized that I was tired of playing second fiddle to her best friend. I felt neglected and jealous."

"My daughter was old enough for me to return to work, so why was I avoiding looking for a job? My therapist helped me see how frightened I am of competing and how horrible I would feel if an employer didn't want me."

EXPLANATION OF HOW

_____ I am interested in learning about the context and sequence in which my problems arise.

"I've begun to keep a food journal, and I can already see that I do my worst bingeing during the lonely times and when I'm afraid."

"Every time I think about leaving my wife, my son gets in trouble in school and I have to stay. My wife just couldn't handle him."

EXPLORATION OF THE PAST

_____ I want therapy to help me think about my life history and my past relationships as a way of understanding myself today.

"I've tried to put the experience out of my mind, but in therapy I'm learning how my father's having sex with me has affected every aspect of my life, from my relationships with men to my functioning in my career."

"It was startling to find out that I don't stay with a woman for very long because I'm terrified of going through the same kind of smothering closeness that my mother gave me as a child."

"Being adopted colored my life in ways that I never considered, especially since my adoptive parents kept it a secret from me. I grew up knowing that something was the matter, but never knowing what."

CONFRONTATION

_____ I want my therapist to bring me face-to-face with aspects of my behavior, thoughts, or feelings that are in contradiction to each other, to what I want, or to what I believe about myself.

"My therapist pointed out that even though I am relieved to be in therapy and find it a help, I show my reluctance by coming late and forgetting to pay him on time."

"No matter what I brought up, he brought it back to my drinking. He showed me how my alcoholism affected everything and everyone around me."

NONVERBAL WORK

_____ I want my therapy to include physical contact and exercises designed to release tension and stored-up feelings, reenact a childhood scene, or provide nurturing.

"I live almost entirely in my head. I talked my way through years of therapy, still blocking my emotions. Doing body work puts me in touch with feelings in a direct way."

"Being in a group where people have physical contact seemed artificial at first. Now I allow myself to take in nonsexual nurturing that is not available anywhere else in my life."

"My previous therapist had told me that I was denying and forgetting things in my past, but actually being there while my psychodrama group played out old scenes cut through my pretense of a perfect childhood. I was stunned."

DIRECTION

_____ I want my therapist to suggest topics for discussion during sessions or to assign things for me to do between therapy sessions.

"We found that setting aside half an hour to talk each day before bedtime, a suggestion from our therapist, started us back on the path to being close again."

◆ Task 3 ◆
Learn About the Schools of Psychotherapy

Just as there are Protestants, Catholics, Jews, Hindus, and Muslims, with various denominations of each, so too there are psychoanalysts, behaviorists, humanists, and family therapists, with various denominations of each. Each has its own theoretical beliefs, rituals, and language. Each approach presents a different theory about how people function and how to help them change. Each has been useful for a number of clients. There is no "right" approach to therapy that will suit everyone. Your personal needs and preferences will suggest the most useful approach for you.

You can learn about the various schools of therapy by:

- Talking to people about their experience in different forms of therapy.
- Reading novels and books about therapy. (See "Resources," for descriptions of helpful books.)

- Going to lectures and workshops sponsored by training institutes, university psychology and social work departments, and individual psychotherapists in your community.
- Attending minithons or marathons (extended group sessions) to sample specific approaches.

This section explains some of the different kinds of therapies. Now that you have decided which therapeutic strategies are most appealing, you can match them to the descriptions of the therapies available (not all of the many available can be presented here). You can then end up with a list of schools of therapy that interest you.

Although they may use other strategies as well, therapists who practice a particular approach to psychotherapy tend to *emphasize* the strategies mentioned after the description of that approach.

Behavioral Therapies

These focus on the treatment of specific behavioral problems rather than on underlying psychological states or processes. Behavior change is seen as a learning process, and therapy has an educational focus. The following approaches share this perspective.

Behavior therapy is short-term and usually focuses on one particular symptom, a troublesome habit, or a series of maladaptive behaviors. Techniques adapted from traditional learning theory, such as positive and negative reinforcement, role playing, modeling and rehearsing new behavior, and the systematic desensitization of anxiety, are used. Behavior therapists often teach clients how to employ techniques themselves. Behavior therapy is used for people with eating disorders, phobias, and behavior problems in children. ISSUE ORIENTED, DIRECTIVE, EDUCATIONAL, EXPLORES HOW.

Cognitive therapy. A more recent modification of traditional behavior therapy, this approach is based on the assumption that feelings and behavior can be changed if ideas are changed. The cognitive therapist focuses his attention on correcting learned misconceptions. Assuming an authoritative stance, the therapist works with his client to clearly define the target problem and to design a specific program to change the assumptions and beliefs that have kept the problem in place. This therapy is particularly successful for people suffering with mild to moderate depression. DIRECTIVE, SUPPORTIVE, CONFRONTATIONAL, EDUCATIONAL, EXPLORES HOW AND WHY.

Body therapies (bioenergetics, core energetics, and radix). Basing their approach on the work of Wilhelm Reich, body therapists believe that emotions are blocked by holding tension in various muscles and that releasing tension expands emotional awareness and leads to character change. In addition to verbal work, body therapists do physical work to alter character structure. Body therapists treat the same range of problems that are treated by traditional talk therapy. NONVERBAL, GROWTH ORIENTED, DIRECTIVE.

Family Therapy

Some schools of family therapy grew out of the individual and group approaches that are described in this section, while others emerged from communication theory and general systems theory. While volumes are written describing, comparing, and integrating the various schools (see "Resources," page 233), three of the most commonly practiced approaches will be described here.

Bowen systems theory. Murray Bowen's work grew out of research with the families of hospitalized psychiatric patients. The therapist assumes the posture of a consultant and usually coaches one member of the family to become his or her own person and to be constructively connected to other family members. With the change in one person there will automatically be a change in the family system. Bowen theory views dysfunction as a multigenerational process and therefore makes use of a genogram—a map of at least three generations of a family—to plan the therapeutic strategy. DIRECTIVE, EDUCATIONAL, GROWTH ORIENTED, CONFRONTATIONAL, EXPLORES WHY, HOW, AND THE PAST.

Strategic therapy (paradoxical or problem solving therapy) is problem focused and change oriented. Changing destructive interpersonal patterns is favored over gaining insight. The therapist actively directs what goes on in and out of therapy, with exercises, prescriptions, and homework assignments that may seem paradoxical. One such paradoxical technique is "restraining change," in which the client or family is warned against changing too fast, with the result that some families can begin to move toward change. This approach is often practiced by teams of therapists working behind a one-way mirror. SHORT-TERM, ISSUE ORIENTED, DIRECTIVE.

Structural family therapy. Created by Salvador Minuchin, this therapy is based on the notion that changes in a family will produce change within the individual. It focuses on structural elements such as boundaries around the individual or around the family as a whole, alliances and coalitions within the family, and the family hierarchy. Working with all available family members, the therapist or therapeutic team will shake up a family structure in order to change it. The therapist is active and authoritative, often working behind a one-way mirror. Minuchin's theory, which emerged from work with economically disadvantaged families, is now used with many kinds of families. DIRECTIVE, ISSUE ORIENTED, EXPLORES HOW, SUPPORTIVE, EDUCATIONAL.

Humanistic Therapies

Concerned with helping people to realize their full potential, humanistic therapies focus on emphasizing the whole person rather than a specific problem or symptom. The present (being) and future (becoming) are the focus rather than the past and causal factors. In addition to the approaches described below, many Jungian therapists consider themselves to be humanist therapists.

Client-centered therapy (Rogerian) stresses the development of self-awareness, leading to self-actualization. The client possesses the necessary resources for change, which will emerge out of a safe, nonjudgmental relationship between the therapist and the client, a relationship that encourages the client to explore thoughts and feelings that had been avoided as too threatening. This interaction between therapist and client is thought to produce growth. GROWTH ORIENTED, SUPPORTIVE.

Existential therapy takes the unfolding of the client's genuine self as its goal. The therapeutic relationship is a real encounter between two people, who are both changed in the direction of greater self-awareness, self-actualization, and wholeness in the process. The therapist does not attempt to explain the client to him- or herself, but rather encourages him or her to explore and confront his or her own experi-

ence in order to define what his or her life is about. GROWTH ORI-
ENTED, SUPPORTIVE, CONFRONTATIONAL.

Gestalt therapy. Created mainly by Frederick Perls, this therapy
may continue for a period of a few weeks to several years. The client is
encouraged to explore his or her inner experience, and how he or she
relates to others and to his or her environment. Gestalt therapy is most
commonly practiced in a group, where one member is on the "hot seat"
and interacts with the therapist, while the rest of the group observes.
The client is helped to reclaim and reintegrate cast-out parts of his or
her self. Spontaneity and the "here and now" are emphasized over
insight and explanations of the past or rehearsals for the future. The
Gestalt therapist uses body awareness exercises, "talking to an empty
chair," and role playing. GROWTH ORIENTED, DIRECTIVE, CONFRONTA-
TIONAL.

Transpersonal psychotherapy supports self-actualization and the
attainment of a higher level of consciousness. Spiritual traditions, including Eastern thought, are often a part of the process. Practitioners
especially recommend this approach for those concerned with exploring their personal values or with finding meaning in life. Increasingly,
it is employed with the terminally ill. GROWTH ORIENTED, SUPPORTIVE.

Psychoanalytic or Analytic Therapies

This group emphasizes gaining insight into and control over unconscious or forgotten feelings, memories, and attitudes that distort
current realities. The next approaches are among the many schools
of psychoanalytic therapies generally practiced in the major U.S.
cities.

*Interpersonal analysis (Sullivanian analysis, the Cultural School
of Psychoanalysis).* This approach emphasizes not only what goes on
within the self but also what goes on between people, which is reflected
in analysis by what goes on between the client and analyst. The analyst
considers him/herself a "participant observer" and may be more active
than other analysts. GROWTH ORIENTED, SUPPORTIVE, CONFRONTA-
TIONAL, EXPLORES WHY, HOW, AND THE PAST.

Jungian analysis (analytic psychology, depth psychology). Client
and analyst meet once or twice per week for a year to a number of

years. Using guided imagery, the Jungian analyst and the client explore the meaning of ancient and modern symbols. The analyst may recommend certain readings (bibliotherapy) and other educational or artistic experiences (visual art, music, and movement). Jungian analysts work with many different kinds of people, including those looking for "enlightenment" and enhancement of their creativity. GROWTH ORIENTED, EXPLORES WHY AND THE PAST, SUPPORTIVE.

Psychoanalysis. Deep personality change is the goal of psychoanalysis. The client investigates whatever comes to mind, including wishes, dreams, fantasies, daily life, and current relationships. The relationship with the analyst ("transference," page 116) can be looked at for the purpose of understanding internal difficulties that hamper the person's growth and cause an inability to work out daily problems. Psychoanalysts believe in giving the client enough time to get into as much depth as possible in order to recapture the deepest experience of the self. The client comes to sessions three to five times a week for from two years to whatever length of time is needed. To enable the client to focus on him/herself without distractions, the analyst sits behind the client, who rests on a couch. GROWTH ORIENTED, CONFRONTATIONAL, EXPLAINS WHY AND HOW, EXPLORES THE PAST.

Psychoanalytically oriented psychotherapy. This is an insight-oriented therapy whose goal is to help the client resolve current problems. Although psychoanalytically oriented psychotherapists use many of the techniques found in psychoanalysis, the therapy is less intensive, shorter in duration, and more focused on specific problems like work and relationships. The therapist actively interprets those aspects of the person's past life and current dynamics that are responsible for the client's difficulties. The client comes to sessions once or twice weekly and may use the couch or sit facing the therapist. GROWTH ORIENTED, SUPPORTIVE, CONFRONTATIONAL, EXPLORES WHY, HOW, AND THE PAST.

Self psychology (the Chicago School of Psychoanalysis, Kohutian analysis) was founded by the psychoanalyst Heinz Kohut. Patients may or may not use the couch. Primarily concerned with fostering the development of a healthy sense of self, these analysts emphasize an empathic, supportive understanding. Kohutian analysts believe that most emotional problems arise because the self is stunted or distorted in its development. GROWTH ORIENTED, SUPPORTIVE, EXPLORES WHY, HOW, AND THE PAST.

Other Schools of Psychotherapy

The following schools do not easily fall into the major categories described above. They are, however, commonly practiced.

Crisis intervention. Crisis intervention is a specialized approach to the treatment of specific, acute crises in which immediate, intensive help is required. Often, a flexible approach to scheduling prevails, in which a client may be seen initially for three hours, say, or twice in one day, according to his special needs. The goals are to mobilize all available resources and to help a person to return to his regular life, doing as well as or better than before. The therapist is active, authoritative, and focused on the immediate situation. DIRECTIVE, ISSUE ORIENTED, EDUCATIONAL, SUPPORTIVE, SHORT-TERM.

Eclectic therapy. Eclectic therapists borrow ideas and strategies from a number of schools of therapy. Disciplined eclecticism is difficult to master. A therapist must learn when and how to apply different approaches to therapy. By asking where he or she has studied, you can assure yourself that a therapist has sufficient training and learn which strategies and schools of therapy are used.

Feminist therapy is an orientation that emphasizes the impact of the role of women in society as an important determinant of a woman's individual difficulties. The goal of feminist therapy is to help women develop a sense of personal and political power. Feminist therapy is most often a perspective brought to the practice of other approaches to therapy rather than an approach to therapy in and of itself. Therefore, no particular set of strategies is associated with this therapy.

Hypnotherapy. A trance state, an altered state of consciousness in which the client is both relaxed and capable of intense concentration, is induced to increase openness to the hypnotist's suggestions. Hypnosis is generally used for stress disorders, pain management, or breaking destructive habits such as smoking or nail biting. SHORT-TERM, DIRECTIVE, EDUCATIONAL, ISSUE ORIENTED, SUPPORTIVE.

Neuro Linguistic Programming (NLP). The originators of NLP studied the communication patterns of powerful therapists like Milton Erickson and Virginia Satir to learn what made them effective. They observed and set down a system of communicating that produces greater openness to constructive suggestions from the therapist or from the client him- or herself. In this approach, the client is thought to possess the resources necessary for change, requiring only the key to gaining access to them. The client is also taught to communicate effectively with others in his life. NLP is applied to a wide variety of problems, including anxiety, troublesome behavior, and difficulties in relationships. It is used with individuals, couples, and families. SHORT-TERM, DIRECTIVE, ISSUE ORIENTED.

Psychodrama. Created by J. L. Moreno, this therapy is usually practiced in a group of clients who, directed by a therapist, enact past and current events and relationships in the hope of reexperiencing, understanding, and working out the feelings surrounding them. Catharsis, insight, and the integration of feelings and new attitudes are the goals of this approach. Some of the more common techniques are role reversal, encounters between parts of the self, and mirroring. Psychodrama is used with a wide variety of people. It may last from a few months to two years. GROWTH ORIENTED, DIRECTIVE, CONFRONTATIONAL, EXPLORES WHY, HOW, AND THE PAST, NONVERBAL.

Transactional analysis (TA). Originally developed by Eric Berne for practice in groups, TA is now also used with individuals, couples, and families. TA emphasizes the interplay between what goes on in one's head and what goes on between people. The language is designed to make complicated psychological concepts accessible, and clients use these concepts in thinking about themselves and fellow group members. The TA therapy looks at present life events in the context of "life scripts," a plan for living developed during childhood. The therapist and fellow group members are active and often use techniques like role playing, homework assignments, and contracts (clear agreements about the goals and focus of the therapy). ISSUE ORIENTED OR GROWTH ORIENTED, SUPPORTIVE, EDUCATIONAL, DIRECTIVE, CONFRONTATIONAL, EXPLORES WHY, HOW, AND THE PAST.

◆

"I found Dr. Frances's understanding, no-nonsense BEHAVIORAL APPROACH *appealing and was pleased that we would focus entirely on my overeating. It took three weeks, while he helped me write down in detail what I ate, when I ate it, where I ate it, and just what was going on with me when I felt the impulse to eat.*

"At first I was embarrassed to let anyone else know about my

secret bingeing. But now I am in his weight-control group, and he follows the same clear program with all of us. It is a relief to talk to other bingers like me, who understand how I feel."

"During the second session, my GESTALT *therapist instructed me to be the wall I had created in my dream. I was to begin by saying, 'I am Ginny's wall,' and then I was to describe myself and what I did for Ginny.*

"I started slowly at first, stating how huge and substantial I was and how important I was to Ginny. Suddenly, overwhelmed by sadness, surprised by the depth of my pain, I began to sob. I need to protect myself by walling myself off from my own feelings as well as from people around me. I want to get beyond my wall to be free."

"I try not to think about my BIOENERGETIC THERAPY, *I just want to do it, so this is hard for me to describe. Bioenergetics is not for the hysterical, fragile, or those in crisis. With a little well-placed pressure and encouragement to breathe, I reexperience everything that I thought I had safely resolved in my previous therapy.*

"In these first months I have cried and yelled more than I had in my whole life. I began to have orgasms that involve every fiber, every inch of my body. I feel different, or maybe I should say I feel, I really feel.

"For the first time I cannot figure out what the therapist wants and how to be a good patient. My body has a direction and wisdom all its own. For the first time I have surrendered to therapy. I am really a patient."

"What struck me from day one was how people talked to each other in my TA *group. I had never heard people being so clear about their own internal worlds and clear about their responses to events and to the other group members. Unlike my family, group members ask for what they want and take responsibility for getting it. They say no to others when they don't want to do something. It's a new world to me."*

"I had just finished talking about my contempt for Al: He seemed incompetent and a turn-off sexually. My PSYCHOANALYST *asked what came to mind when I think of the bright, charming, and*

attractive Al that I had described just last week. I tried to figure out why my feelings about Al had changed so radically. Then this melody played over and over again in my head—it was 'We Won't Be Fooled Again,' by the Who. I started to sing some of the words: 'meet the new boss, same as the old boss . . .' I was furious and cried as I remembered that when I was six, my father, a charming sailor who I adored, told me that he wouldn't be able to see me for a while because he had to go to sea. When I was eight and still hadn't seen him, my aunt told me he was living with another woman, just forty miles away. As I thought about my father and Al, I realized the depth of my distrust of men."

◆

Complete this statement:

The following approaches to therapy appeal to me because

◆ **Task 4** ◆
Learn About Couple, Group, and Family Therapy

When we think about psychotherapy, we usually think of individual therapy. It is the most common mode of therapy, familiar and comfortable for most of us. Yet other modes, by themselves or in combination with individual therapy, may work well for you.

Group therapy provides a special, safe setting in which to explore your issues with the help of both a therapist and other clients. Group therapy encourages people to communicate openly and give one another feedback. Most schools of therapy, including Gestalt therapy, Transactional Analysis, behavior, cognitive, psychodrama, and psychoanalytic psychotherapy, have their own approach to group therapy.

Most people find that being with others who share common problems is a powerful experience. Seeing firsthand that others have overcome a seemingly insurmountable difficulty can help to create the optimism needed to change. Group therapy can be less costly than individual therapy.

Consider group therapy if:

- You have continuing difficulties in friendships or love relationships.
- You are aware of an issue that comes up between you and your colleagues, supervisees, or superiors at work.
- You feel frightened of social situations.
- You are uncomfortable with some of your behavior with others.
- Others have complained about your behavior, and you are unclear about what upsets them.
- You are puzzled about what makes other people tick.
- You have a hard time speaking up about what you are thinking and feeling.
- It is difficult for you to work out differences that come up with other people.
- You question your capacity to be a loving, caring person.
- You believe that your problems are unique and that you are alone with your difficulties.
- You are lonely.

◆

"My therapy group is like the good family that I did not have as a child. I don't like all the members, but I care about them and what happens to them."

"Sometimes I love my group because of the incredible support and understanding I get. Then there are the times I could disappear into a hole when they confront me with my stuff."

◆

Group therapy (interests) (doesn't interest) me because

Couple therapy. Although many relationship problems are helped in individual therapy, on the whole, couple therapy is more successful with this kind of problem. Couple therapy can help with married, unmarried or separating couples, gay or lesbian couples, business partners, friends, and divorcing and divorced parents.

Check the statements that apply to you.

_____ My partner doesn't listen to me.
_____ I am dissatisfied with our sex life.
_____ We fight over little things.
_____ We can't find time to do fun things together.
_____ I can't tell my partner how I'm feeling.
_____ We keep to ourselves too much.
_____ Our sex is routine.
_____ We don't talk things out.
_____ I feel distant from my partner.
_____ We don't like the same friends.
_____ I can't tell my partner when I want sex.
_____ We don't enjoy things together.
_____ My partner doesn't understand me.
_____ We don't support each other.
_____ We're mad at each other a lot.
_____ It seems useless to discuss things.
_____ I want to leave this relationship in a civilized way, without causing unnecessary pain.
_____ I feel lonely when we are together.
_____ We have to work together better as parents.
_____ We don't share responsibility.
_____ I am disappointed in my marriage.
_____ Our fights get violent.
_____ My partner nags me.
_____ My partner is critical of me.
_____ One or the other of us withdraws under stress.

◆

"I can't figure out why our couple counseling works. Nothing that dramatic seems to happen. Yet I see that we are doing better. Maybe just having a chance to talk calmly and getting a better understanding of each other is what we need."

"After my boyfriend and I split up for a week, we decided to give couple therapy a last-ditch try. It was hard work for ten months, but we did it. We married last year and now I'm thrilled to be pregnant. I am so grateful we tried it."

"We had the worst divorce imaginable. Now we meet monthly with a therapist to discuss the best ways to raise our daughter."

◆

I think couple therapy might work for us because

Family therapy.   Family therapy comes in a variety of forms; the entire family may attend each session, or, at the other extreme, only one or two members of a family may be seen at any one time, to be coached by the therapist about dealing with the rest of the family. (See page 42 for descriptions of some of the major schools of family therapy; page 233 in "Resources" will direct you to more detailed information.)

How can you know if your family is in trouble and needs therapy? The following list reflects the ideas family therapists have about families who could profit from therapy together.* If you identify with these statements, family therapy can help.

Check the statements that describe your family.

_____ The parents don't work together.
_____ One parent joins the child(ren) against the other.
_____ Parent(s) and child(ren) are alienated from each other.
_____ Parent(s) and child(ren) can't make decisions together.
_____ Parent(s) and child(ren) are not respectful of each other.
_____ Child(ren) get in the middle of parents' fights.
_____ Family members are emotionally distant.

* The checklist for deciding on the need for family therapy is based loosely on material from the Timberlawn Psychiatric Research Study as found in Lewis, J. M., W. R. Beavers, J. T. Gossett, and V. A. Phillips, *No Single Thread: Psychological Health in Family Systems.* New York: Brunner/Mazel, 1976.

_____ There is little spontaneity.

_____ There are too many or too few rules.

_____ The child(ren) often end up taking care of other family members.

_____ Family members blame one another.

_____ Family members do not respect one another's privacy.

_____ Family members talk at rather than to one another.

_____ Family members don't understand one another.

_____ Outsiders are viewed as untrustworthy.

_____ Family members are suspicious of one another.

_____ Parents are dissatisfied with their marriage.

_____ It is hard to get anyone to acknowledge change in a family member.

_____ Family members spend a lot of time escaping into fantasy.

_____ Family members are hostile to one another.

_____ There is no joy in the family.

_____ Family members are cruel to one another.

_____ The family feels hopeless about the future.

_____ Family members cannot comfortably spend time away from one another.

_____ Parents behave like children rather than like responsible grown-ups.

◆

"We fought all the time and could hardly stand to be in the room together. We've come a long way."

"I couldn't get my four-year-old daughter to cooperate with the simplest requests, so in desperation I took her to a family therapist. During the first meeting, the therapist told Ella to leave the room and said that the problem was that I acted like the child and looked to Ella to see what I should do. She gave me an assignment to do every day to let Ella know that I had the authority."

"No one knew how to fight or how to disagree. We had to be coached, like learning to play tennis, move by move."

◆

I think family therapy may be appropriate for us because

If you think that couple or family therapy makes the most sense for you, yet the others involved are unwilling to participate, do not give up. Contact an appropriate therapist or agency and make this reluctance the first order of business. You can be seen alone and, with the therapist's assistance, plan a way to bring the others into therapy with you.

◆ Task 5 ◆
Decide What You Will Look For

Now that you have a picture of your ideal therapist, the kind of therapy you might like, and the various options that are important to you, it is time to sort out the preferences that are most important to you. These preferences are the ones that you will be looking for as you conduct your search for a therapist. Do keep in mind the preferences that are interesting but not crucial. If you find a therapist who has these as well, they will be extra benefits to weigh in his or her favor when it comes time to decide between therapists.

THERAPIST PREFERENCE CHART

As you review each section of the chapter, complete the appropriate part of this chart below to reflect your personal needs and preferences.

**Personal Qualities
and Background**
(PAGES 28–30)

**Professional Experience,
Specialty, and
Credentials**
(PAGES 31–34)

**Therapeutic Strategies
Emphasized**
(PAGES 37–40)

**Therapeutic Approach
Used**
(PAGES 40–49)

**Individual, Group,
Couple, or Family Therapy**
(PAGES 49–54)

The chart will be used for guidance when you start your actual search for a therapist, in the next chapter. You can refer to the completed chart when you phone and then meet prospective therapists.

•4•

Finding Your Therapist

TASKS

---

1. Consider Your Options
2. Collect Three Names
3. Interview the Therapists
4. Choose Your Therapist

♦ Task 1 ♦
Consider Your Options

Now that you have a fairly clear idea of what you want in a therapist, how do you go about finding a person who meets your qualifications? The first thing you need to know is whom to ask and where to look.

If you are in a personal crisis, you may feel a sense of urgency about locating a therapist right away. Consult the Resource section at the back of the book for the addresses and phone numbers of nationwide referral organizations to help you begin your search as soon as possible.

If you are able to take more time, you can develop a list of potential therapists in several ways. Generally, asking for personal recommendations is the best approach. A friend, a co-worker, a family member, your physician, or a religious leader may have the names of therapists or clinics with reputations for compassion and competence.

However, you may not be in a position to get a personal recommendation or the recommendations you have gotten may not include a therapist who meets your qualifications. In that case, there are a number of other routes to finding a good therapist. You can contact a professional organization, a training institute, your employee assistance program, or a local hospital or clinic and ask for the names of several

WHERE TO FIND HELP IN AN EMERGENCY

If you need help immediately, your phone book is often your best guide to the resources available in your area. In the front of most *telephone books* you will find a special section with community service numbers. You may find numbers for: *alcoholism and drug abuse counseling, child abuse and maltreatment reporting, domestic violence, battered women's shelters, runaway hot lines, mental health services, rape crisis hot lines, crisis intervention, suicide prevention hot lines.* Every county in the United States has a crisis service.

In an emergency, simply *call the operator by dialing 0 or 911* and explain the nature of your problem; you will be given an appropriate number to call or be switched directly to a service that can help you.

Or go to the *emergency room of the nearest hospital* for assistance.

therapists with whom you can schedule a consultation. "Resources," page 227, contains information to help you find a therapist who will have the qualifications, training, background, or expertise you are looking for.

Let's get down to some specifics about what else you may want to consider in locating prospective therapists.

Settings

Psychotherapists can be found in both private and nonprivate settings. The therapist in private practice is free to work out arrangements that are mutually agreeable regarding such issues as fee, frequency and number of sessions, and focus of treatment. Although usually more costly than therapists in nonprivate settings, many therapists have a sliding fee scale.

Set up as for-profit or not-for-profit institutions, private clinics can provide a variety of services and can specialize in particular problems, such as phobias, substance abuse, or family relationships. Some clinics are connected with private inpatient hospital facilities. The costs vary considerably, from expensive to moderate.

Generally, a nonprivate setting offers lower fees and a wider variety of services under one roof than any one private psychotherapist can provide. Nonprivate settings can offer individual, group, family, child, and couple therapy. There may be a waiting period before you see someone, you may have little choice over whom you see, and sometimes there is a limit on how long therapy can last. Within these limitations, excellent psychotherapy is often offered in the following settings:

Training institutes have two purposes: to provide psychotherapy services and to train and supervise people learning a particular school of therapy (Transactional Analysis, behavior therapy, psychoanalysis, family therapy, Gestalt therapy, Jungian analysis, etc.). If you are interested in a specific school of therapy and there is a limit to how much you can afford, an institute may be a good source for you. (See "Resources," page 227, for suggestions.)

University clinics. Many graduate schools of psychology or social work sponsor clinics which train students while providing inexpensive therapy to the community. These students tend to be less experienced than institute trainees. However, they are usually carefully supervised, hard-working, and enthusiastic. A student may be available for only the academic year, September through May.

Mental health clinics can be found in hospitals, community mental health centers, and family agencies. A clinic that is part of a hospital will be at least partially staffed by psychiatric residents (M.D.s in training to be psychiatrists) who usually leave the clinic within a year. Often, very experienced clinicians (usually psychiatrists, clinical social workers, or clinical psychologists) work alongside newcomers and may be able to stay with a client for longer periods.

Social service or family service agencies. These agencies are primarily staffed by professional social workers, along with some psychologists and psychiatrists. Students may provide some of the services. These agencies may have specific requirements for eligibility and restrictions of the length and kinds of services offered.

Returning to Your Former Therapist

If you have had previous experience in therapy, you may be wondering whether to go back to your former therapist or start again with someone new. Here are some guidelines to consider in making your decision.

Consider returning to your prior therapist if you can say:

My experience was positive and
_____ I need only a few sessions. My former therapist will be able to get right down to work without having to get to know me first.
_____ I am feeling fragile or am in a crisis. My former therapist may be able to zero in quickly on what is troubling me.
_____ I am in the midst of issues that my former therapist dealt with in the past and I think that I can learn more from him or her about it now.
_____ I have no good reasons for starting with someone new.

My experience was mixed and
_____ I have moved from therapist to therapist without solving my problems.
_____ I have some unresolved issues with my former therapist that I would like to clear up.
_____ I have noticed that the same difficulties I had with my therapist are occurring with other people too. I'd like to sort out what part I may have played in the difficulties between the two of us.

If, after consideration, you find that you have doubts about returning to your former therapist, check to see if any of the following apply to you.

I am
_____ feeling like a failure because I need therapy again.
_____ afraid that my therapist will be disappointed in me.
_____ unsure if my old therapist's approach will be useful with my current problems.

_____ harboring feelings of anger, distrust, or disappointment that I didn't resolve during therapy.

_____ angry that I am having a recurrence of old difficulties.

_____ avoiding painful issues that were raised before in my therapy.

Consider seeing a new therapist if you

_____ Had a negative and unproductive experience before.

_____ Think that you could use a new way of looking at yourself.

Complete these sentences:

When I think about returning to my former therapist, I

The advantages and disadvantages of seeing a new therapist are

◆

"My therapist was so proud of the progress I'd made, it's embarrassing to be a mess again."

"I left therapy before my therapist thought I was ready to end. If I go back now it feels like I am admitting that I was wrong."

"I was never sure that Tom was pushing me as hard as I needed and felt like I was getting away with something. I think that working with someone else will tell me more about what was me and what was him."

◆

If you've decided to return to your former therapist, turn to Chapter 5, "Getting Off to a Good Start." Otherwise:

◆ Task 2 ◆
Collect Three Names

Just as it is unwise to become engaged after dating only one person, so too it is usually unwise simply to choose the first therapist you meet. If you have been in therapy before, you may have some basis for comparison, but if you are new to therapy, it is useful to visit more than one therapist. Then, having experienced a session or two with two or three therapists, you can think about how you might work with each of them. Seeing more than three therapists is usually too confusing.

Once you have collected a few names, you can use the telephone to narrow your list to the most promising possibilities:

Use the Telephone to Gather More Information

It's natural to feel uncertain and perhaps anxious as you make your first calls. Check your Therapist Preference Chart, page 55. It can remind you of what you are looking for and enable you to eliminate an unsuitable therapist on the telephone.

Here are some questions you may wish to ask:

- Are you accepting new clients?
- Where are you located?
- Do you have hours (before work) (afternoons) (evenings) (weekends)?
- What is your fee? Is there the possibility of a reduced fee?
- Do medical health insurance companies cover your services?
- Do you charge for an initial consultation?
- Do you work with _____ (special issue or group) (couples) (families) (groups)?
- Can I be seen _____ (number of times per week or month)?
- What are your credentials and training?
- Or _____

If you are calling clinics, you may also want to ask:

- Do you see people who live in _____ (name your part of town, since some clinics have geographic limitations)?
- Is there a waiting period before I can be seen?
- Are there income restrictions on receiving your services in your clinic? (Some places have a ceiling on the income of clients eligible for their service.)
- What kinds of training do the therapists in your clinic have?
- Can you send me any literature describing your services?

• Is it possible for me to request a therapist who is _____
_____

(Use your Therapist Preference Chart to describe.)

Consider the Nitty-Gritty
Before Scheduling an Appointment

Before you schedule a visit to a therapist or clinic, there are some more or less mundane matters to consider about what you learned on the telephone.

CAN I AFFORD THE FEE?

There is a great deal of variation in the cost of psychotherapy. The fee charged depends on what part of the country you live in, the therapist's training and reputation, and whether the therapy is individual, group, couple, or family.

You do not necessarily get the best therapy by paying the highest fee. Fees are determined largely on the basis of custom, with men and medical doctors getting the highest fees and women and nonphysicians getting the lowest.

These are typical hourly fees:

M.D. psychiatrist	$80–150
Ph.D. psychologist	65–120
M.S.W. clinical social worker	35– 75
Group psychotherapy	20– 50
Family and couple therapist	50–125
Clinic	0– 80

Figure out whether the fee is manageable on a regular basis. If it is not, do ask before your visit whether a fee reduction is possible.

CAN I GET THERE ON A REGULAR BASIS?

Consider the location of the clinic or therapist. Is it close enough to work or home that you can reasonably expect to keep appointments? If not, you might want to make an appointment with another therapist or clinic whose location or schedule better accommodates you.

WHAT KIND OF RECEPTION DID I GET OVER THE TELEPHONE?

The kind of welcome you receive on the telephone is one of the variables you can take into account in deciding whether to meet a particular therapist. Although therapists and clinic receptionists are busy and may not be able to speak at length on the telephone, it is reasonable to expect that your call will be handled with tact and courtesy and that the person will be able to answer your basic questions. If you feel negative about the reception you received, consider making some more calls before scheduling an appointment.

I Will Schedule Appointments with

1. Name _____
   Address _____
   Telephone _____
   Comments _____

   _____

2. Name _____
   Address _____
   Telephone _____
   Comments _____

   _____

3. Name _____
   Address _____
   Telephone _____
   Comments _____

   _____

◆ Task 3 ◆
Interview the Therapists

When we are feeling uncomfortable, unsure, and upset, it is hard to imagine having the resources to interview a therapist. Although this kind of interviewing may feel like an unwanted burden, it is not as difficult as it may sound. It is meant to encourage you to ask questions and to be aware that whether you see a particular therapist or not is *your* choice to make.

This first visit, considered a *consultation,* is your chance to talk about yourself and about therapy without making a commitment actually to engage in therapy. It is an opportunity for you and the therapist to interview each other. Just as you will be trying to decide if the therapist can be helpful to you, the therapist will be trying to decide if he or she can help you. You will both be looking for signs of rapport. Do you feel comfortable together? Is there basic agreement on important matters?

Since this is a time for collecting information, tell the therapist about yourself. He or she may ask you specific questions or may let you take the lead and offer information. In either case, these are some of the basic areas that may be covered.

- *What do you want from therapy?* What is bothering you and when did these problems begin? Why are you looking for help now? What have you done so far about your concerns? What do you hope to accomplish in therapy?
- *Who are you?* The therapist will want to know basic biographical information as well as your current status. Are you married? With whom do you live? Do you work or go to school?
- *How are you managing?* What is your work life like? Is there anything getting in the way of your functioning as well as you can? What are your relationships like with your friends, lover, or spouse?
- *What is your outlook on yourself and the world around you?* How do you feel about yourself? How do you experience the important people in your life?

Be sure to let the therapist know if you are having any of the serious problems in the Emergency Symptom Checklist, page 22. Even if you find it difficult to talk about, let the therapist know what is troubling you from the very first session. You will want to make sure that this therapist can offer you the help you need and will start dealing with your problems immediately.

Prepare Your Questions

To prepare for the consultation, review Chapter 1, "Taking Stock," to remind yourself of the issues you want to raise. You (or you and your partner, if you are going to see a couple therapist) can prepare by responding to the next statements.

I want to remember to tell the therapist about

I want to ask the therapist

Although one consultation may not allow enough time for all your questions, check off the questions below that you want to ask. If you have checked a lot of them, rate them in order of importance.

_____ How do you see my problem?
_____ Do you think you can help me?
_____ How can therapy help me?
_____ How do you usually work?
_____ Do you have training and/or experience with _____ ?
_____ Have you worked with people like me?
_____ If I need to be seen with my (parents) (husband) (children), will you see us or will you refer us to another therapist?
_____ How long is each session?
_____ Can you arrange for tranquilizers or antidepressants if I need them?
_____ What are your professional qualifications?
_____ What are your policies regarding missed sessions or vacations?
_____ What is your fee, and is it negotiable?
_____ Are you covered by medical insurance?

CLINIC SETTINGS

The First Phone Call. Usually you will be asked a number of questions on the telephone to determine whether you are eligible for the services offered by the clinic. Eligibility often depends on where you live, how much money you have, or whether the clinic provides the service you need. If there is a sliding scale for fees, you will be asked to bring verification of your income and possibly your expenses. You may want to ask whether there will be a waiting period before your initial interview, and how long the usual time span is between an intake interview and the beginning of therapy. If the waiting time is longer than you think you can manage, say so. They may be able to accommodate you sooner or suggest a clinic with a shorter waiting period.

The Intake Interview. The purpose of an intake interview is to explore the issues that bring you to therapy in order to see if this particular clinic is suitable for you and, if it is, to decide which of the programs offered will best address your needs. The more information you can give the interviewer about what brings you to therapy and what you are looking for, the more likely you are to get what you want. Be sure to tell the intake worker what is important to you so that you can be assigned to the most compatible therapist.

The intake worker is unlikely to be assigned as your therapist. In some settings the intake worker has leeway in assigning therapists and can consider meeting your requests.

Meeting Your Therapist. After the intake procedure is completed, there may be a waiting period before your first meeting with your therapist. Think about any new questions you would like to ask your therapist.

If this is not the first time you have been in therapy, share this during the consultation. You'll want to describe:

- Your previous therapy
- The reason you began therapy before
- When it took place
- How long it lasted
- How frequently you were seen

- Whether you were in group, individual, couple, or family therapy
- What was useful and what was not
- Any difficulties with the therapy
- The reason you left therapy

At the end of the consultation, you will have some idea of what it would be like to be in therapy with this therapist. You may be sure that you don't want to work with him or her. You may need a second consultation with him or her before you decide. Or you may be sure that you can work together.

◆ Task 4 ◆
Choose Your Therapist

Since a good fit between therapist and client is the critical ingredient for success in psychotherapy, only you can determine if you have found the right therapist. Your instincts are your best guide. You do not need to decide how good a therapist is, but rather how well the two of you can work together.

Sometimes it is clear from the first session or two; things just click and you work together smoothly. Conversely, you may dislike or feel uncomfortable with your therapist from the first session, and your inability to get beyond this interferes with working on anything else. Sometimes clients find themselves in between, cautious about trusting their therapist at first and then, gradually, coming to a greater ease at working together.

Signs of a Good Fit

Check those statements below that reflect your thoughts about each of the therapists you interviewed. Use a separate column for each therapist.*

---

* The concept of the importance of good fit between therapist and client informed the development of this checklist and is derived in part from "The Helping Alliance Questionnaire" in Luborsky, L. *Principles of Psychoanalytic Psychotherapy.* New York: Basic Books, 1984.

THERAPIST

1	2	3	
☐	☐	☐	This therapist seems interested in me.
☐	☐	☐	I am interested in the way this therapist does therapy.
☐	☐	☐	I expect good results.
☐	☐	☐	I believe that I could learn to trust this therapist.
☐	☐	☐	This therapist seemed genuine and sincere.
☐	☐	☐	He or she listened well.
☐	☐	☐	I started to like this therapist.
☐	☐	☐	This therapist seemed skillful.
☐	☐	☐	We had good rapport.
☐	☐	☐	This therapist seemed to understand.
☐	☐	☐	He or she was helpful.
☐	☐	☐	I was comfortable with this therapist's personal style.
☐	☐	☐	I learned something new about my problems.
☐	☐	☐	What I want fits with what this therapist has to offer.
☐	☐	☐	I think that I can work with this therapist.

◆

"I was prepared to like Ralph before I ever saw him, because he was my girlfriend's therapist first. Whenever she told me something that he said to her, I thought it made a lot of sense. I liked the changes she had made in her life. I was predisposed to like him, and I did."

"As I described why I needed help, I began sobbing. 'I've ruined my life. I work from eight in the morning until ten at night. I never relax. I have nothing for myself.' After a pause, he said, 'You can change that.'"

"He was a slob and the office was a mess. I was so relieved. I felt at home."

"In the first session with Judy, I was running through my history in therapy, which consisted of lots of kinds of therapy with different therapists. She said that she saw a pattern of my not finishing things and wondered if I didn't leave just when serious work might get started. She said she'd work with me only if I agreed to stay for at least a year. I agreed and I'm glad. She picked up on a central problem right away."

*"The main thing he did was to let me set my own pace; I've been
so watched over and controlled my whole life that I really needed
to feel like I could do it my way."*

◆

A Mixed Reaction

You may find yourself in between, having a mixed reaction about a
therapist. Complete whichever of the following statements apply:

Although I didn't like

I did like

I was unsure about

I was uncertain about learning to work with this therapist because

Perhaps you need more time to decide.   Some people find making
a choice about a particular therapist easier after a trial period of therapy. You and the therapist choose a period of time to evaluate your
mutual suitability. Usually, six sessions is a good amount of time for
sampling a particular therapist. An alternate route is to interview more
therapists, seeking someone about whom you feel more certain.

GROUP, COUPLE, AND FAMILY THERAPY

In individual therapy, your relationship with the therapist provides the medium in which growth can occur, while in group therapy you have to evaluate your fit with the group as well as with the therapist. Before beginning group therapy, you may meet the therapist alone for a number of sessions so that the two of you can get to know each other. You can ask the therapist to suggest a time frame for an evaluation period, after which you can decide if the group is useful.

Couple and family therapy present a different challenge. It is not always necessary or possible to locate a therapist with whom everyone in the family feels equally comfortable. Initially, you may need to rely on the therapist's credentials or on the reports of satisfied clients in making your selection. After a number of sessions, you will be aware of changes in your relationships within the couple or family which will help you decide if the therapy is working.

Signs of a Poor Fit

Sometimes no therapy is better than bad therapy. If you identify with any of the statements below, definitely continue your search.

_____ I have no confidence that this therapist can help.
_____ The therapist talked about him / herself in a way that had nothing to do with me or my therapy.
_____ The therapist seemed to be prejudiced against my class / ethnic or racial background / age / sex / sexual orientation.
_____ He or she promised a quick, easy solution to my problems, requiring little effort.
_____ I felt afraid and unsafe.
_____ The therapist had goals for me that I have no interest in.
_____ There was no rapport between us.
_____ I didn't think the therapist liked me.

IF YOU HAVE RESERVATIONS ABOUT AN ASSIGNED OR CLINICAL THERAPIST

If your first couple of sessions with your therapist left you with mostly negative feelings about him or her and a pessimistic sense of your therapeutic future, let the therapist know that you believe you could work better with someone else. This may be difficult, but if you stress that you are concerned that the two of you make a poor fit and not with any issues of competence, it may go easier. He or she may agree, and you will be reassigned to another therapist.

Most clinics require that you try a few more sessions before being assigned to a new therapist. Although clients usually do well when they are reassigned, some clinics are surprisingly rigid about transferring clients from one therapist to another. In this instance, you will have to decide whether it is possible to struggle on to be reassigned, to accept the therapist and work on the negative aspects of the fit, or to find a therapist elsewhere.

_____ I have a bad feeling about this therapist.
_____ I can't imagine ever trusting this person.
_____ The therapist seemed to have no idea what he or she was doing.
_____ The therapist judged me or put me down.

Generally, you can trust a strong impression formed during your initial consultation. Feeling optimistic that therapy will help, sensing that a therapist is understanding and dependable, feeling that you are engaged in a joint effort and share similar ideas about the nature of your problem, are the beginnings of the good working relationship necessary for successful therapy.

Don't dismiss a negative reaction to a therapist. If your instincts tell you that this person is wrong for you, trust yourself. It is worth the time and effort to locate a therapist who elicits more positive feelings in you.

♦

"I was so anxious and upset. Talking brought some relief, but I didn't feel a connection between us. She had a good reputation, yet I found her difficult to reach, tense, and remote."

"I could not get comfortable sitting in the living room. I felt like I was supposed to be a member of the family, not a client. The therapist seemed likely to be too friendly and to lack authority."

"My wife gets the name of the most famous family therapist in the city and loves her. I do not feel helped at all and won't go back. So she finds another therapist, this one's not as famous, just moderately well known. This time I like her and my wife feels like the therapist sees only my side of things. This is getting to be a big deal. I say that we never agree on anything, that's part of our problem. But we go to a third man, not famous and not primarily a family therapist at all. We both like him; he's gentle, takes time with both of us. It paid to keep looking."

♦

If No Therapist Seems Right

If you interviewed a number of therapists and have negative reactions to all of them, something more may be going on. Take the time to consider why you may be having difficulty connecting with any therapist right now. Do any of the following questions fit your situation?

_____ Could I still have some lingering doubts about my need for therapy?

_____ Are my fears about therapy intruding into the selection process? (Turn back to page 24 and review the therapy reservations list.)

_____ Do I have a general pattern of mistrust or indecisiveness that I am bringing to this situation?

I may be having trouble deciding on a therapist because

Once you have considered the possibilities, schedule another appointment with the least objectionable therapist and discuss your reservations. Exploring your reservations with a therapist may help to overcome them or may validate your need to continue your search.

◆

"Maybe I was looking for Dr. Ruth. I could not settle on a sex therapist for us. Finally, after number four, my girlfriend put her foot down. We went back to one she liked and talked about my trouble finding a therapist. He thought my indecision was connected to my sexual problems, being perfectionistic in everything I do."

"I just know that any therapist I go to will tell me to cancel, or at least postpone, the wedding. I think that's what's keeping me from actually deciding on a therapist."

"My lawyer told me to go see a shrink because she thought it might be taken into account before the judge sentenced me for selling cocaine. At the hospital out-patient clinic, the therapist talked so softly that I could hardly hear her; I almost had to fall out of my chair to catch her words. She looked so young that she couldn't know much about life. So I asked for someone different. This little bald guy with glasses and beard walked into the room; I thought, 'Here we go again.' But this guy was something else. First thing he says, 'Don't try to con me. Don't show up for one hour a week, not work, and expect a good report to the judge. I'm here to work; if you are too, fine. Otherwise, forget it.' I never would have guessed that a doctor like him would know where I was coming from."

◆

If You Have Little Choice

The ideas in this chapter are most useful if you have the option of selecting your therapist. But you may have few options from which to choose. You may live in an area where few therapists are available; you may have limited financial resources; you may have only one therapist available to you; or you may be so desperate to begin therapy immediately that shopping around is impossible.

If you experience a poor fit with your therapist and have no choice but to continue, be up-front about your reservations and discuss them with your therapist. Therapists want to be effective, and it may be possible for him or her to address your concerns. You can also choose to keep the therapy short and focused on your immediate problems. When your situation changes, you can locate a more compatible therapist with whom to work.

Make a Decision

Reread your impressions about each therapist you have met.

I have decided to see _____ because

You can use the information in the next chapter to make the most of your therapy.

·5·

Getting Off to a Good Start

TASKS

---

1. Explore Your Reactions to Beginning Therapy
2. Establish a Good Working Relationship
3. Develop Your Therapy Goals
4. Make a Commitment to Therapy

Like the first few months in a new school, therapy takes some getting used to. You will be finding your way as you get to know how your therapist practices his or her craft. You will begin to get a sense of how this experience may work for you.

Now that you have chosen a therapist, you can start the important task of building a good working relationship. If all goes well, you will begin to trust your therapist, start to feel engaged in therapy, and develop an understanding of how you can use therapy to achieve your goals.

There is no one right way to begin therapy. Each therapy experience is as unique as a fingerprint, and, like a fingerprint, each course of therapy follows a generally established pattern. Together, you and your therapist will work out the specifics of your therapy.

◆ Task 1 ◆
Explore Your Reactions
to Beginning Therapy

We all experience complex emotions as we begin this journey. On the one hand, we may welcome the opportunity to have someone really listen. We may feel challenged or supported, calmed or enlightened.

At the same time, it may be uncomfortable to reveal ourselves in the ways that therapy encourages. Even after beginning therapy, it may be difficult to accept that we need help or that we will change in the process.

Below are statements made by beginning clients. Think about the sessions you have had so far and check those statements that reflect your experience.

_____ I am encouraged by what my therapist says.
_____ I dread going to therapy.
_____ Therapy is more intense than I expected.
_____ I'm embarrassed about the way we fight in our couples' session.
_____ I feel understood and accepted by my therapist.
_____ I think my therapist is pushing me to do things his or her way.
_____ I wonder what my therapist is thinking.
_____ I think my therapist likes me.
_____ I am challenged to try new things.
_____ I am relieved to get things off my chest.
_____ I can't seem to get my point across.
_____ I'm afraid the couples' therapist likes my partner better than me.
_____ I'm beginning to figure out what's expected of me.
_____ I don't like getting so upset.
_____ I believe therapy is helping me already.

What I like about therapy so far is

What I don't like about therapy so far is

◆

"My therapist focuses so intently on me that I can almost hear her listening. She is quiet when I would expect any other person to talk, and she talks when I least expect it."

"I want my husband to change first; then I'll change."

"It's like torture for me. I've always kept to myself and relied on my own resources. It's hard to believe that anyone could or would want to help me. I'm not sure that therapy will work. It feels like a leap of faith into a cold void."

"I'm afraid the therapist will ask me embarrassing questions in front of the kids."

"Once I told her all about my problems, I got this blank feeling. Now what am I supposed to do?"

"After I leave sessions I keep mulling things over. It's fascinating to get a fresh point of view of my life. Somehow I feel better."

◆

Styles of Beginning

We tend to develop predictable ways of doing things and to repeat them in therapy as we do elsewhere. If you get to know the way you usually begin things, you can learn to handle your new therapy in the best way possible. The next exercises will help you become aware of any patterns of beginning that you have with new people or new activities. Check the statements that apply to your style of beginning.

When I begin a new relationship or activity, I
_____ jump in quickly, ignoring any reservations I have.
_____ move in cautiously, taking time before I reveal myself.
_____ trust slowly before I make any commitments.
_____ try hard to make a good impression.
_____ feel shy and keep to myself until I feel comfortable.
_____ am very quick to be critical of what is going on.
_____ become involved and stay that way.
_____ become involved and then lose interest easily.

_____ am concerned that I might get trapped.
_____ start out with high hopes and get disappointed.
_____ am different depending on the situation.

In responding to these next statements, think of a project or job you've started or how you usually begin a relationship with a new friend, teacher, co-worker, or boss.

I notice these similarities and differences between my usual style of beginning and how I am beginning therapy

If I use my past patterns to predict how my therapy will go, this is what I might expect to do next in therapy

I might be able to increase the likelihood of a good beginning for my therapy if

◆

"I get very enthusiastic about anything I start. Then I get bored and move on. Sure enough, I started therapy with a bang and now I want to leave. My therapist helped me to not leave therapy too soon. She suggested that I try to work out my dissatisfaction with the superficial relationships in my life by staying in therapy even though it is hard for me."

"My therapy group is helping me see how the way I started my therapy group is like I start other things, jumping in over my head without much concern for consequences. In the first sessions I spilled my guts and got involved in other group members' problems without knowing what I was doing."

◆

Use Your Journal

You will get more out of therapy sessions if you take the time to pay attention to your thoughts and feelings, dreams and fantasies. A journal, begun in this early phase of therapy, will help establish a habit of self-observation that will be helpful as you work on yourself during and after therapy.

Your experience of therapy will change and evolve. A journal will allow you to check in with yourself from time to time and express your thoughts and feelings about beginning therapy. You can use the journal to wind down after a session or to record thoughts and feelings that you forgot or weren't able to say during a session. You can use this material to help you prepare for future sessions. After a while you will notice how your reactions to therapy have changed and how and where you have made progress.

◆

"It was the third month of therapy, and I wrote down my first dream since therapy began. The atmosphere was dark and dangerous and there was a huge, heavy door like a combination of a door to a dungeon and a bank vault. I pushed it open just enough to see a small boy curled in a ball in the corner, sobbing. I slammed the door shut. My therapist asked me if the dream reminded me of my feelings about therapy. As I thought about it, that seemed right; last time we talked about my past, and therapy was starting to feel scary. I wasn't so sure that I wanted to keep looking at things."

◆ Task 2 ◆
Establish a Good
Working Relationship

The most talented therapist cannot do the work of therapy without a good working relationship with his or her client. The relationship provides the context for repair and growth. Your relationship must have the potential of developing into one that is strong enough and positive enough to sustain you through good times and bad.

While the therapeutic relationship resembles other good relationships, here are some ways that it may differ:

THE RELATIONSHIP IS NOT RECIPROCAL

Unlike other relationships, where you may take turns giving and taking, the relationship with your therapist is focused on you and your needs. It is not your job to take care of your therapist.

◆

"I usually take on the role of the helper with my friends and family. Now, with my therapist, it feels strange; I'm not used to being on the receiving end. I miss that sense of competence and control."

"It's so delicious to have a whole hour just for me."

◆

YOUR THERAPIST IS THE EXPERT

Your therapist has seen people use many different ways of coping with problems. He or she is trained to listen, to understand, and to tolerate your feelings, thoughts, and behavior. He or she has resources of knowledge rarely available to others. It is not realistic to expect friends and family, however well-meaning, to have the same skills and resources as your therapist.

◆

"I am surprised that my therapist knew exactly what was going on with me and my wife. He told us straight out that he didn't think fighting was our real problem. He said that we argue all the time because we are scared of being close to each other."

◆

YOUR THERAPIST HAS MORE POWER

In this relationship, each partner is equal in dignity, while one, the therapist, has special expertise and primary responsibility for defining the rules and limitations. Initially, it may seem that you have the problems and your therapist has all the answers. Issues of the difference in power and status between you may be apparent to you. Over time, your therapist can help you to take on the power in your therapy and in your life.

◆

"I guess I want someone to take over for me. I wish she would run my whole life."

"He seems to be pulling rank, telling me what I am thinking and feeling. I feel like an emotional illiterate."

"I have never been asked to think so hard about myself, to take so much responsibility for what I say and do. Yet I've never before been treated so respectfully."

◆

THE RELATIONSHIP HAS LIMITATIONS

You may be aware of limitations in this relationship that are not commonly found in others. You are expected to show up at a particular time, which may not be the time when you experience your need most intensely. You meet in a special place, perhaps a clinic or an office, which may not be the place of your choosing—you might prefer a walk in the park or a quiet corner of a coffee shop. You have to pay a fee. You may or may not be free to call the therapist between sessions. The limitations provide the boundaries to protect this intimate yet professional relationship.

Your therapist is also limited with you in ways that he or she is not with friends and family. Therapists must bring their professional selves to the session, making sure that their own problems do not intrude.

In order to provide a helpful perspective for your benefit, therapists try to be as objective as humanly possible. They are not involved in your everyday life to the extent that they become dependent on you for love and friendship. Unlike family and friends, your therapist has no stake in keeping you the familiar person whom they know and love. This is one reason why many therapists avoid socializing with their clients.

◆

"I'm so upset right now that I have trouble lasting between sessions. Sometimes I sit by the phone for hours and wonder if it's all right to call my therapist."

"It seems so strange that my therapist won't see me perform at my recital, when we worked so hard together to make it happen."

◆

YOUR THERAPIST IS BOUND BY CONFIDENTIALITY

An important protection is provided by the legal and ethical expectation that a therapist may not reveal anything about you or your therapy without your written permission. There are exceptions to confidentiality. For example, child abuse must be reported to the authorities. Therapists may also be subpoenaed in certain legal situations, like child custody cases. You may want to discuss this issue further with your therapist and perhaps consult a lawyer.

◆

"It was hard for me to believe that Dr. Delano wouldn't tell my mother that I was skipping school, but he never did. It was a different story when I told him about trying to kill myself. He said he couldn't keep that kind of secret, not when it was a matter of life and death."

"I was scared my husband would be able to use the things I said in therapy against me in court. Even though I need to talk to someone bad, I couldn't take a chance on losing my kids. So my therapist said I should check with a lawyer to see exactly what laws apply to my situation."

◆

Your Therapist's Responsibilities

You and your therapist are partners, and each of you has responsibilities. You can expect your therapist to provide a safe place where your thoughts and feelings can be expressed without fear of retaliation or abandonment, where nothing is so bad that it cannot be discussed. Your therapist will listen carefully to both your spoken and your unspoken story and will try to understand your experience and help you reach your goals.

Your Part in Establishing a Good Working Relationship

As the other partner in this relationship, you have responsibilities as well. You come, you participate, and you pay your fee. Yet you can do more to help the therapy go deeper or faster. A good therapeutic relationship is central to the success of therapy. Learning about what you can do to help establish a solid partnership with your therapist can put you ahead of the game. The next section offers guidelines to help you create a strong working partnership with your therapist.

♦ *Let yourself be known.*   Talk about your thoughts, feelings, and behavior as openly as possible. There is no magic in therapy, and no one can read your mind. Your therapist can know for sure only what you describe and demonstrate about yourself. Letting yourself be known can yield the good feelings attached to being understood and the likelihood that your therapist will be more engaged and better equipped to help you.

Some subjects, such as sex or money, are hard to discuss. You may not want your therapist to know about your bad temper or how far behind you have fallen at work or school. You may feel ashamed of the fights you are having with your partner. Ultimately, exploring these avoided areas will provide you and your therapist with clues about the kind of help you can use.

You may be concerned about your therapist's reactions; perhaps you fear disapproval. There's no reason for you to trust automatically, but nothing will convince you like testing his or her responses. If you are having trouble revealing your thoughts and feelings, talk about this difficulty.

It may take some time before you are comfortable enough to share yourself fully. Go at your own pace. Don't push yourself, but don't hold yourself back if you are ready to share more.

♦

"No one knows when I'm upset. People see me as lucky and special. I get compliments about how cheerful and terrific I am. It

is taking me months to tell my therapist that I am depressed and feel like giving up. I am afraid he won't like me if he knows about this sadness."

◆

Complete the following sentences.

I was relieved when I was able to tell my therapist

At this time it is hard for me to tell my therapist

I feel this way because

◆ *Listen to what is said.* In the beginning you may be too upset, too frightened, too eager to talk, or even too angry to attend carefully to your therapist. Give yourself the time to consider how what was said might fit for you.

Are there specific times when it is hard for you to listen to your therapist? Is it especially difficult when your partner in couples' therapy or your fellow group members speak to you? Let your therapist know what makes it hard for you to listen. See if you can figure out why it is hard to listen to what is said. Check any of the statements below that reflect your difficulty in listening.

_____ It's such a relief to get things off my chest that I don't want to stop talking.
_____ I think I am being criticized.

_____ The (therapist) (group) say complicated things that I can't understand.

_____ I don't want to hear criticism of anyone I care about.

_____ The comments seem to suggest that my problems are bigger than I thought.

_____ I don't want to be told what to do or how to think about myself.

_____ I am frightened by what is said.

_____ I think that I am being misunderstood.

_____ I don't think that my (therapist) (group) like me.

_____ I don't trust my (therapist) (group).

_____ I am afraid to change.

_____ I think that (he) (she) (they) are saying that I am (choose one or more): (angry) (guilty) (bad) (inadequate) (dumb) (self-involved) (indecisive) (jealous) (competitive) (spiteful) (sad) (crazy) (hopeless) (rigid) (unlovable)

_____ or, _____

• *Ask questions.*   Asking questions is a corollary of listening carefully. Human communication is so complex that it is unreasonable to expect every effort to be perfectly clear. Don't hesitate to ask for clarification or suggest that your therapist repeat what he has said in different words. If you are confused about anything said or done in therapy, do ask about it.

I have these questions about my therapy so far

These questions occur to me when I think about what my (therapist) (partner) (group) member said or did

• *Attend to what you want from your therapist.*   It is important to figure out what you want from your therapist and to keep track of any changes in what you believe you need. While some of what you want may turn out to be possible, and some may not, your expectations are useful material to discuss with your therapist. Check any of the statements below that reflect your expectations of your therapist.

I'd like my therapist to
_____ calm me down.
_____ help me define my problems.
_____ listen while I get things off my chest.
_____ unburden me.
_____ help me to feel better.
_____ help me solve my problems.
_____ tell me what to do.
_____ take care of me.
_____ understand me.
_____ straighten out my partner.
_____ love me.
_____ make sense of my life.
_____ accept me.
_____ keep me in line.
_____ open me up.
_____ keep me from going crazy.
_____ expand my awareness.
_____ be there for me.
_____ control my destructive behavior.

If you are in couple, family, or group therapy, do this exercise again. This time check what you would like from the others involved in your therapy.

I would like my (partner) (members of my family) (therapy group) to

I wish my therapist would

I am glad my therapist

 • *Give your therapist feedback about therapy.* Giving ongoing feedback about how therapy is working is an important contribution that you can make to its success. Therapists start out with educated guesses about how to proceed, but it is your feedback that teaches your therapist how to work with you and your particular needs. Although sharing all your reactions may not work out in your social or work life, your feedback, both positive and negative, increases the effectiveness of your therapy.

Something your therapist suggests may seem sensible or seem to come from outer space, may confuse you, touch you, or seem unrelated to what you are saying. Something said may cause you to question your therapist's standards or indicate that he or she knows very little about your background.

You may not want to appear critical or tactless in this new relationship, but it is important that your therapist have feedback, even if you feel awkward in the process. Mentioning your concern about how you give feedback can itself become a useful part of your therapy.

If you are unsure about how to give your therapist feedback, the following examples may be helpful.

◆

"I felt anxious when you were silent. I imagined that you were judging me."

"When you said that my mother had been harsh with me, I was upset. I don't want you to blame her for my problems."

"I was relieved when you suggested how I could handle my son's homework, because I was having trouble thinking through a solution on my own."

◆

Write a sentence or two of feedback that you could give your therapist about something that happened recently. You may want to choose something your therapist said or did that was especially useful to you or something that was difficult or painful.

I want you to know that

Have I told my therapist my thoughts and feelings about therapy so far? If not, is it because
_____ I don't want to hurt my therapist's feelings.
_____ I'm afraid I will make my therapist angry with me.
_____ It's awkward to be so grateful.
_____ I want to be more certain about what I think before saying anything.
_____ I don't want the therapist to get the idea that I am complaining.
_____ I feel uncomfortable telling him / her all the things I like about therapy.

◆

"I told the therapist that I wanted her to be direct with me about what she thinks. I am not some fragile flower who will fall apart. Well, she heard me; therapy has been intense since then."

"I told my therapist that I was feeling bruised and battered from being confronted so much. He asked me if this feeling reminded me of anything, and I remembered how my father used to line us kids up for beatings. I could sense how moved he was as I described my father's cruelty. Since then I feel that my therapist is really on my side."

◆ Task 3 ◆
Develop Your Therapy Goals

As you allow your therapist to get to know you, your hopes and fears, your problems and pain, you will find some new ways of looking at yourself and your life. As you develop a new perspective, you will also see new ways that you can use therapy.

In the beginning phase, you and your therapist will come to an understanding about how therapy can help you. With this understanding, you can continue to learn more about what to do in your role as a therapy client and what you can expect from therapy.

Here are some examples of how clients start to develop a new perspective on what brought them to therapy. They began to see more specifically how they could use therapy. Those words underlined are the client's current therapy goals.

◆

"I always thought that the problem in my marriage was my husband's passivity. It drives me nuts. To my surprise, the couples' counselor focused on how I interrupt my husband and take over. We have decided to use therapy to work on learning how to be cooperative with each other. I have to stop taking over and my husband has to try to be more assertive."

"It amazed me to learn that my depression was what my therapist called an 'anniversary reaction' to the death of my brother several years ago. I see that I never really dealt with my feelings about his death. Therapy will be the place for me to explore my feelings and make peace with my brother."

"I couldn't have been more certain when I entered therapy that I was going to focus all my attention on my problems with work and my boss. Yet when I did this, my therapist pointed out how I was behaving at work as though I was still a ten-year-old kid, so cautious and terrified that my father would hurt me again. I'm frightened to remember all that pain, but it seems like I'm reliving it anyway. My therapist says that if I don't <u>confront these painful memories and understand their impact on me</u>, *I will just repeat the old patterns, at work and elsewhere."*

"My boyfriend said that I was so plastic and polite; it looked like I was acting all the time. I was frightened that I had no feelings. My therapist pointed out that I stopped myself from feeling at some point. He said that I should <u>study those times when I turned off my feelings</u>. *He said that way I could* <u>learn why I stopped myself</u> *and what I was feeling."*

"The most helpful thing the therapist said was that the humiliating love affair my husband had with a fellow teacher did not mean the end of our fifteen-year marriage. She said that my husband was really devoted to our relationship and had the affair to get me to pay attention to how really serious our problems with sex are. It helped me to stop playing the outraged wife so we could <u>begin to look at our sexual problems</u>."*

◆

What Do I Want from Therapy?

You may have some ideas about what you want for yourself, yet you may be unsure about how therapy can help you achieve what you want. Part of what happens in therapy is translating personal goals into goals that can be achieved in therapy.

If your personal goal is to feel better about yourself, therapy can help directly. If, on the other hand, your goal is to be a successful artist before your thirtieth birthday, therapy can help only indirectly: You have to get the necessary training and practice in your art, while therapy can help clear the obstacles if you are somehow getting in your own way.

Reread the goals that you formulated on page 17. If you were unsure of your goals then, the process of making goals for your therapy can stimulate your thinking.

Imagine that you have finished therapy and you are pleased with what you have accomplished. What has changed, and how is your life different?

Return to the present and think about how therapy might help you bring about the changes you want.

How can therapy help me with what I want to accomplish?

Reach an Understanding with Your Therapist

Since therapy is most successful when client and therapist are on the same track, talk to your therapist about your therapy goals. See if they are in accord with what your therapy has to offer.

Circle the statement that applies to you and use the space provided to write more if you wish.

My therapist (clarified) (changed) (accepted) (questioned) my therapy goals

My therapist and I have reached an understanding that I will use therapy to

• *Therapy goals change over time.* What you have just written are your therapy goals. Since the process of setting and fine-tuning goals continues throughout your therapy, these goals can change as your needs change. As you and your therapist understand more clearly the issues involved, you may see new ways that you can use therapy.

Therapists differ in the way goal setting is used in therapy sessions. Some therapists make specific, clear, and sometimes written contracts with clients about the goals for therapy. Contracts usually have a behavioral component, so that both therapist and client will know when the contract has been fulfilled. Contracts made with behavioral and TA therapists may include the steps necessary to achieve the therapy goals.

Psychoanalytic, humanist, and other therapists believe that therapy is a process in which both sought after and unexpected growth occurs. Thus, in sessions with these therapists, clients "go with the flow" of the therapy, spontaneously responding to the process. Goal setting may be referred to on occasion but is not a focus of the therapy.

◆ Task 4 ◆
Make a Commitment to Therapy

Whether it takes a few weeks or a number of months, you will know when the beginning phase of therapy has been completed. You will feel comfortable about making a commitment to be in therapy with the therapist that you have chosen.

Can I Begin to Trust My Therapist and the Therapy Process?

Now that you have had the opportunity of firsthand experience, you are developing a feel for your therapist's particular approach. If things are going well, you are developing trust in your therapist and the therapy he or she practices. This beginning trust will help you to involve yourself in the process of therapy.

You may spend most of your time talking with your therapist in a way that seems close to an intense conversation with a helpful friend, or you may be trying out new behavior or techniques unlike anything you have experienced in your daily life. Perhaps you are searching for meaning in your dreams and fantasies; keeping close track of when and how much you overeat; pounding a pillow and giving voice to your angry feelings; telling your partner about your unspoken doubts about your relationship; having an imaginary conversation with someone with whom you are in conflict; or pretending you are the part of yourself you do not like.

Initially, some of the things your therapist asks you to try may seem absurd. Within reason, of course, if you can lend yourself to the process, you will have a chance to know whether a particular technique can help you.

I believe I (can) (hesitate to) (can't possibly) (am beginning to) trust my therapist now because

I (understand) (am confused by) (disagree with) the techniques used in my therapy because

I might be more trusting toward my therapist now if

Do I Still Have Reservations About Therapy?

Look back to page 24 and review the reservations you had about therapy before you started. Are any of them still with you? Are you more comfortable now, or have you developed new reservations?

I am hesitant about making a commitment to this therapy because

Any reservations about therapy may make it difficult for you to make a commitment to the process. Be sure to bring this up with your therapist.

When I discussed my reservations about therapy with my therapist

Unless you have serious doubts about whether you and your therapist can work well together, you can still go forward even though your reservations are unresolved. Discussing your concerns can be a valuable part of your therapy.

If, after discussing your reservations thoroughly, you continue to have doubts about your therapy, reread this chapter to see if you can figure out what is standing in your way. (Turn to Chapter 9, "Evaluating Your Therapy," for a guide to use with your therapist in deciding what may be going wrong.)

Can I Make a Commitment to Therapy?

If you have settled many of your reservations and still cannot decide to commit yourself to your therapy, you may be struggling with some difficulty about making a commitment in and of itself. Examine your feelings and thoughts about committing yourself to an intimate relationship or a major project. Sometimes old patterns of distrust or fears of closeness can stand in the way.

Describe any difficulty you have had in making commitments in the past. What is (similar) (different) about the situations?

Take a Step Forward

By the end of the beginning phase, you have had a number of new experiences. The Beginning Phase Checklist below will help you see what remains for you to do before you move on to the middle phase of therapy. If you cannot check off any particular item, review the chapter.

BEGINNING PHASE CHECKLIST

———— I have a good idea about what to expect from therapy.
———— I understand what my therapist expects of me.
———— I believe that I have made myself understood.
———— I believe that my therapist is trustworthy.
———— I have made sure that we are working on my most serious problems.
———— I have begun to see myself or my problems in a different way.
———— I know how therapy can help me.
———— I believe my therapist is on my side.
———— I believe that my therapist is competent.
———— I believe that my therapist can help me.
———— I made a good decision when I chose my therapist.

If you put a check next to all of these items, you are ready to continue your journey into the middle phase of psychotherapy.

•6•

Therapy Etiquette

Guidelines for Manners in Therapy
Questions and Answers About Therapy Etiquette
Exploring Ground Rules
Special Ground Rules for Group, Couple, and
    Family Therapy

By now you have probably noticed that therapy often turns generally accepted rules of decorum upside down. Your therapist may encourage you to discuss topics like sex and money, point out inconsistencies in your behavior, or boldly inquire about the intimate details of your life. Therapy can also encourage you to behave in ways that might be outrageous or unacceptable in another setting. You may be asked to say whatever pops into your mind without regard to propriety, to yell so loudly that the neighbors could hear, or to talk openly about feelings of hatred and lust.

This combination of unusual expectations and permission to break certain generally accepted rules of propriety does not mean that "anything goes" in therapy. Therapy provides us with the opportunity for new experiences within a clearly defined structure governed by ground rules and a considered therapeutic plan. Doing the unfamiliar is designed to alter your usual patterns of feeling, thinking, and behaving, and, thus, to open up possibilities for growth.

"It's all grist for the mill" can be considered an important principle in psychotherapy. This means that whatever we think, feel, or do can be used to further our therapy. Therefore, even small, seemingly insignificant events and reactions can be viewed as communications to be studied and understood, leading to interesting, and often unexpected, discoveries.

◆ Guidelines for Manners in Therapy ◆

IT IS ALWAYS APPROPRIATE TO

- Ask your therapist any question.
- Give your therapist feedback.
- Be informed about any of your therapist's ground rules or policies.
- Refuse any treatment strategy.
- Keep your therapy as private as you wish.

Etiquette During Sessions

ASKING YOUR THERAPIST PERSONAL QUESTIONS

At times you may find that you are wondering about your therapist's personal life. Your questions may be a matter of curiosity or may seem crucial to you.

Therapists differ in their responses to personal questions; some therapists are reticent about personal issues, others are expansive. For theoretical reasons, some therapists will respond to personal questions by asking a question of their own. You may hear: "What is your fantasy about the question you have asked?" or "How will it help you to have that information?" These questions are attempts to help you look more deeply within yourself, to keep the focus on your thoughts and your fantasies. This can also be a way for you and your therapist to understand transference reactions (see pages 116–117). Other therapists will use material from their personal lives to illustrate a point, to encourage you, or to suggest how you might handle a situation.

◆

"My therapist talks about what it has meant to her to be an adult child of an alcoholic. She is willing to answer my questions about

*how she has overcome so much. Her openness and bravery mean a
great deal to me. I know that if she can do it, so can I!"*

*"I was terribly disappointed to learn that my therapist had been
divorced twice. I felt sentenced to the same fate and worried that
he couldn't help me. I couldn't believe that I could manage that
part of my life better than he could. I wish I didn't know about it
so that I could preserve my ideal version of him."*

◆

BEGINNING SESSIONS

The beginning of a session marks the transition from the everyday
world to the special time when we are free to concentrate on ourselves.
How you begin your sessions may vary, depending on the intensity of
the issues that you are focusing on and the cues you receive from your
therapist. Much can happen in the moments that begin the therapy
session.

The beginning of a session is hard for me when

◆

*"I can always tell when I'm avoiding a painful issue; I begin by
talking about everyone else and not myself."*

*"When I have not seen my therapist for a while, it takes me about
half the session to reconnect. I report on what's happened in my
life until I am ready to move into doing some more powerful
exercises that will get me into heavy feelings."*

*"We always seem to have a fight on our way to our couples session
and need to begin by clearing the air."*

◆

SILENCES

Many people feel uncomfortable about silences in therapy. Yet
silences differ. Some silences feel angry or punitive, whereas others
feel comfortable and contented. As with most aspects of human behavior, there can be many reasons for silences.

Are there silences in your sessions? See if you can identify with one or more of the following ways of understanding them:

- The silence can be a way to show your therapist some aspect of your experience, like what it felt like for you to grow up in a family feeling alone and disconnected, or how depressed you are.
- It can be a part of a power struggle between you and your therapist. You may feel that the therapist wants you to produce, and for some reason you do not want to do that for him or her. It is hard to see that it is really for *you*.
- Speaking may feel like the first step toward altering a part of your life that you are not sure you are ready to change.
- You may find that you have nothing to say on a day when you are avoiding talking about something difficult in your life or in your feelings toward your therapist.
- Silences may feel soothing. There are not many people with whom you can share the intimacy of a silence. You may find yourself feeling safe and peaceful during a silence.

If you are uncomfortable with the silences, talk about your discomfort. Think out loud. Try to remember if you ever felt the same way before. Let it be part of your therapy.

ENDING SESSIONS

Ending the session is a sensitive issue for many. It is the moment when you may be reminded most forcefully that this is a professional relationship. Noting how your sessions end and how you respond to ending may yield unexpected information.

Endings are hard for me when

When the therapy session ends, I often (check any that apply to you)

_____ wish my therapist had warned me, so that I could prepare.
_____ am relieved.
_____ seem to be cut off by my therapist.
_____ feel upset about being dismissed.

_____ react as if I'm being abandoned.
_____ want more time.
_____ wish *I* would end the sessions.
_____ or, _____

    There is no right way to end every session for every client. Therapists differ in their degree of skill in handling endings. Some therapists look pointedly at their watches, some give a five-minute warning, some abruptly announce that the time is up. To complicate things further, therapists are as casual or exact about time as anyone else. You and your therapist may be a good or poor match on this issue. With some discussion, you and your therapist will probably be able to work out a way of parting that takes your needs into account.

◆

"When time is up, I leave as fast as possible. When I don't, I start to feel like a thief taking what's not mine."

"Eleanor said that I always tell her these crucial things about myself just as I am leaving a session. She calls it doorknob therapy."

"As the session is about to end, my therapist's tone of voice changes. She says 'uh huh' more frequently. It's like a song she sings to alert me that there isn't much time left."

"My therapist lets some people ramble on forever and then cuts the rest of us off at the end of the group session. I found this really annoying. After I brought it up, we all decided to become a lot more conscious of time and make sure that no one was left out."

◆

Etiquette Between Sessions

MAKING REFERRALS TO YOUR THERAPIST

    If your therapy is going well, you may want to share your therapist with a friend or relative who needs help. You may also want to give your therapist the gift of a referral.

    Recommending your therapist to someone else may or may not

work out. You may find that your therapist does not accept referrals from clients or that your feelings about sharing your therapist are problematic. Some therapists believe that working with clients who know each other always causes unnecessary complications; others allow referrals after some exploration or even encourage referrals, making any issues that emerge grist for the mill. If your therapist declines the referral, he or she will probably suggest the name of another therapist.

As I think about recommending my therapist to someone I know, I realize that

_____ I want to give my therapist something extra to show my appreciation.

_____ I don't want the complications of sharing my therapist with anyone I know.

_____ I hope my therapist will change the person I'm referring to suit me.

_____ I value my therapy and want the person I care about to have a good experience too.

_____ I'm afraid my therapist will like the other person better than me.

_____ or, _____

◆

"Several of my friends go to my therapist. We have a common language and way of viewing ourselves that is really useful."

"It's embarrassing to admit it now, but once when I was really mad at Dr. D. I referred him this very difficult co-worker of mine. I knew she'd give him a hard time."

"I came from a family of twelve kids, and I never had a thing that I didn't have to share. When I realized how jealous I felt about my sister working with Lisa, I decided against it."

◆

WAITING ROOM ETIQUETTE

The waiting room is a place where everyday etiquette is practiced. Some issues can come up while you are waiting for your appointment to begin, and your reactions to what happens there can become a part of your therapy. What happens as you wait for your session to begin?

If I hear a part of someone else's session, I

If my session is over and I meet another person in the waiting room, I

◆

"I couldn't hear what they were saying, but I did hear laughter and animated conversation. I thought that my therapist likes him better than me. Then I thought: It serves you right for listening!"

"I love talking with fellow group members in the waiting room before the session. We gossip about our therapist—which college his kids go to, where he goes on vacation, what kind of tennis player he is, what his wife looks like. It's not exactly therapeutic, but it's fun."

◆ Questions and Answers About ◆ Therapy Etiquette

FORMAL VS. INFORMAL STYLE

Q. *I have been in therapy twice and each time it's been so different. The first time, I called the therapist "doctor," met in an office, and I never learned anything personal about him. My next therapist asked me to call her by her first name. We met in her home, and she used herself and her family to illustrate her points. Is one approach better than the other? How do therapists decide what to do?*

A. A formal or an informal style in and of itself is not associated with a positive outcome to therapy; what is important is forming a solid working relationship with your therapist. For some people, a therapist's style may contribute to developing a sense of comfort and trust. (See page 67 for more information on assessing the fit between you and your therapist.)

Your therapist makes choices about how formal or informal to be with you, based on theoretical considerations and on his or her personality and preference. Even the smallest decision may be based on theoretical considerations; time has been spent in training programs to help therapists think about whether to hand a client a tissue or wait until he asks for one.

Therapists differ as well in how they want to be addressed. Do you have a preference? If so, let your therapist know and ask what he or she prefers. If he or she calls you by your first name, feel free to do the same.

CHANCE ENCOUNTERS

Q. *I ran into my therapist on the street. It seemed so awkward. How should I handle it if it happens again?*

A. A simple hello is fine. Discuss your thoughts or feelings about the meeting with your therapist. Remember, once you are together in a therapy session, it's all grist for the mill.

SOCIAL CONTACT

Q. *It turns out that my therapist and I know a number of the same people. It seems inevitable that we will meet socially. Should I see someone else?*

A. If you and your therapist travel in the same social or professional circles, both of you need to consider how comfortable you would be seeing each other outside of sessions. Therapists' policies about socializing with clients vary, so it is hard to predict how your therapist will respond.

You may want to be reassured that your therapist will be scrupulous about observing confidentiality. You may also want to consider how it might affect you to know the details of your therapist's life. If you do decide to proceed, perhaps you can develop a plan together to minimize any potentially uncomfortable situations.

PROFESSIONALISM

Q. *My therapist got really mad at me last session. Is this professional behavior?*

A. All therapists are human and have their own reactions to a client. Responsible therapists know how to use their reactions to understand you better and to sort out the realistic from the unrealistic in their responses. Therapists use resources like consultations and supervision with another therapist or personal psychotherapy to deal with their reactions and to correct their mistakes.

Your therapist may err on occasion and overreact, misunderstand, misinterpret, or retaliate. Discuss this with your therapist; your solid therapeutic relationship can help to see you through. You can expect your concerns to be taken into account, listened to, and understood, even if your therapist is angry.

Keep in mind what a poor role model your therapist would be if he or she were perfect. Therapists are best when they can give a firsthand demonstration of how they handle their own errors, mistakes in judgment, and bad days.

Assuming your therapist isn't always angry, occasional anger can be therapeutic. Clients can learn how to deal with another's anger, can learn what they do that causes anger, and can learn that a relationship can survive conflicts. If this kind of reaction occurs frequently, it may be a good idea to talk to your therapist about the idea of scheduling a consultation (see page 166), to get another therapist's advice about how to resolve your conflicts.

KEEPING SECRETS

Q. *We have been seeing a marriage counselor for two months now, and I think that he should know that I am involved with another woman. I keep hoping that my wife will be sick or out of town so that I can tell our therapist about it. Should I write or call him? How should I go about giving him this information?*

A. The fact that you are in couple rather than individual therapy needs to be taken into account before you do anything. In individual therapy, your therapist would be responsible only to you. If he learned about your affair, he would be discreet, and the therapy could proceed without a hitch. In couple therapy, your therapist is responsible to both you and your wife. Many therapists believe that their effectiveness is compromised if they join one member of a couple in a secret. It is wise to find out your therapist's position before sharing something that you do not want your wife to know about.

Take the time to think about your motivation in wanting your couple therapist to know about your affair. You may feel guilty and want to unburden yourself. You may be planning to leave your marriage and want your therapist to help prepare your wife for the separation. You may want someone to see things your way and to be on your side or to tell you to stop your involvement because it is destructive to your marriage.

Seeing an individual therapist is a possible solution to your problem. You would have a chance to discuss this issue with some-one who could help you to sort out what's going on without com-plicating your couples' work.

INTERRUPTIONS

Q. *My therapist answers the phone during my sessions. I don't like it. What should I do?*

A. Constant interruptions can disrupt the process of therapy itself and make it difficult to accomplish your work. Disruptions should be kept to a minimum, but even the most protective setting will have occasional distractions.

Talk with your therapist and let him or her know that you do not like having the phone answered during your session. You can expect your wishes to be discussed and taken seriously, even if there is a reason that he or she cannot comply. You may also want to explore your responses, especially if they are intense or seem to be more than is called for in this situation.

TOUCHING

Q. *I am going into a group next week. My therapist tells me that the group does exercises that include physical contact. The idea of touching other people during therapy is confusing to me. How can I tell if it is appropriate?*

A. You are not alone in your confusion. Therapists differ on the therapeutic value of physical contact. Whereas some therapists use touch to discover and alter patterns of feelings, other therapists believe that psychotherapy is primarily a talk therapy; touch is not one of the methods used. Therapists who do use physical contact as a therapeutic tool suggest the following guidelines:

- Anyone involved with physical contact should be free to discuss it at any time: if it is appropriate, how it feels, whether it is helpful.
- Anyone is free to refuse any physical contact that he or she does not want.
- Any physical contact is for the client's benefit, not for the benefit of the therapist.
- In therapy, physical contact should never be for sexual purposes.
- Physical contact is not used to quiet difficult feelings in a way that interferes with the work of therapy.

THERAPY TALK

Q. *Some of my friends talk about every detail of their therapy, while others never mention it at all. How can I decide whom to tell and what to tell them?*

A. Like all aspects of your life, therapy is private; it belongs to you. You can make thoughtful choices about whether or how to share any part of it with the people in your life.

Some therapists believe that talking about therapy with others will dilute important feelings and may undermine your work. What is most important is to be sure to share your thoughts and feelings about therapy with your therapist.

Discuss your worries with someone outside your therapy situation if you suspect that there is something inappropriate going on. (See page 166 to evaluate whether you need a consultation.) Or you may find that you can help integrate what you are learning in therapy by talking about it with a good friend or your partner.

Telling a person about your therapy may produce some surprising reactions, reactions that reveal more about the other person's own hopes, fears, and prejudices about therapy than about you.

PROFESSIONAL JARGON

Q. *My therapist says I am "resistant." I'm not sure what he means, but I don't think I like it. Does that word have a special meaning?*

A. From time to time you may find that you feel disinterested in exploring aspects of yourself in therapy. Your disinterest may mask a fear of facing painful memories or realizations. Some therapists call this disinterest "resistance."

  While many therapists and clients find that this term criticizes more than it explains, it continues to be used.

  If your therapist uses this or any other jargon, be sure to ask what is meant and share your reactions if you don't like it.

MEDICAL INSURANCE

Q. *I want to use my medical insurance to help me pay for therapy. How can I make sure my boss doesn't find out that I am in therapy?*

A. There are two things you can do to help preserve your privacy. You can telephone your medical insurance company and see if you can send your completed forms directly to them. If this is possible, your employer will be bypassed.

  Your therapist can help protect your privacy further. Insurance forms require your therapist to describe your condition. Instead of using words to describe your problem, your therapist can use the numbered code found in the *DSM III* handbook that most therapists use.

  Although many people prefer that their employer not know about their therapy, there may be more for you and your therapist to explore about your reaction. You may find that your concern about your boss reflects your own feelings of shame about being in therapy.

GIFT GIVING

Q. *I want to give my therapist a Christmas present. Is it appropriate?*

A. It depends on your therapist's policies about accepting gifts and on what giving the gift means to you. Clients give therapists all kinds of gifts: a precious secret, a referral, something homemade, something bought. Each of these conveys a different meaning at a different point in your therapy.

Whether or not your therapist accepts your gift, your impulse to give it is grist for the therapy mill. Gift giving, like other behaviors, is a way of communicating, and your effort to understand the message will be useful.

As you talk with your therapist, you may be surprised to learn that your motives are more complicated than you thought:

- You may be impelled to give your therapist a present when you have had angry or lustful fantasies about him or her.
- You may feel tempted to make a referral when you are having secret thoughts about leaving.
- You may believe that your therapist deserves more compensation than his or her fee for putting up with you.
- Perhaps you believe that he or she is soliciting something extra.
- You may find it easier to give a gift than to talk directly about your gratitude.
- You may want your therapist to like you or to think that you are special.

None of these motives cancels out the generosity of your wish, and your therapist needs to make an effort to recognize and acknowledge all the parts of your communication. You should never feel that a gift, or anything beyond the payment of your fee, is required.

As Sigmund Freud said, "Sometimes a cigar is simply a cigar." You may merely want to give your therapist a token of your gratitude.

◆ Exploring Ground Rules ◆

There are ground rules that establish the business side of your relationship with your therapist. If your therapist is in a private practice, he or she will set ground rules based on theoretical considerations as well as on his or her individual personality and style. If you are in a clinic setting, your therapist will have very little to say about the ground rules, as they are set by administrative policy and reflect the clinic's overall approach to therapy.

Some therapists clarify each of their policies at the onset, while others let the discussion of their rules evolve over the course of therapy. The way the rules are implemented varies too. Some therapists are very firm about rules and have a take-it-or-leave-it stance, while others are very flexible about their ground rules and may be open to changing them. Whatever your therapist's school or style, expect a willingness to explain the reasons for his or her ground rules.

LATENESS, ABSENCE, AND RESCHEDULING

Occasionally, events beyond your control may make it impossible for you to get to a session. Your baby-sitter becomes ill, your boss schedules an emergency meeting, or your car breaks down. What happens to your therapy time if you are late or unable to keep an appointment?

Many therapists treat the therapy session as time and space that you have leased. You can use it or not; it is yours and you are expected to pay for it. This is done in part to protect their income (since extra clients are not lined up for the same time) and in part to encourage your continuing commitment to the therapy process.

Depending upon your therapist's ground rules, your session may end at the same time it usually does or be extended if you are late. If you miss a session, you may find that your therapist tries to make up the time or may not be able to reschedule the session. Some therapists will not charge for missed sessions if a certain amount of notice is given.

My therapist's policies are hard for me when

One fruitful area for exploration is what your behavior is saying if you are often late or absent. Check any of the statements below if you identify with them.

I may be late to therapy or miss my session(s) because
_____ something is going on in my therapy that is hard to talk about.
_____ I don't plan well and am often late or miss appointments.

_____ my relationship with my therapist is getting too intense; maybe I need some distance.

_____ I don't like the way therapy is progressing.

_____ I am upset about something (my therapist) (partner) (fellow group member) said or did.

_____ I resent going to therapy to please someone else.

_____ we haven't been focusing on what's most important to me.

_____ I'm feeling too depressed or anxious to get to my appointment.

_____ or, _____

◆

"We figured out that my being late was a way of expressing resentment that I was afraid to discuss. Like a slave, I feel so overwhelmed by authority that I don't rebel openly. I find other ways to do it."

"My therapist told me it was not necessary for me to apologize for my absences. She said, 'Let's spend our time trying to understand them.'"

◆

MONEY

Whether we are clients or therapists, many of us have a hard time talking about money. Bringing up the subject of finances, particularly in the context of the deeply personal issues that are discussed in therapy, may seem jarring or indelicate. Yet your relationship with your therapist is based at least in part on a financial understanding, and being clear about the money part of therapy can prevent future misunderstandings.

Many therapists are flexible about fees. If you are seeking a fee reduction, talk about your income and expenses and present a proposal about how much you can afford to pay. Some therapists are receptive to creative suggestions, including: bartering goods and services; paying for a first weekly session in full and reducing the fee for subsequent sessions; owing some part of the bill until a specified time. If your therapy takes place over the course of years, you can expect periodic increases in the fee, rather like annual raises.

Therapists vary also about payment schedules and charging for missed appointments. Does your therapist expect to be paid at every session, at the same time every week or month, at a time that is convenient to you, or whenever a bill is sent?

The money part of therapy is hard for me when

◆

"I wonder if my therapist resents it when I spend money on myself, since he lowered my fee."

"My therapist told me she was raising my fee, and I was shocked. I thought we negotiated the fee in the first session and that was that. I resent the increase. It's hard to think about this relationship as part of my therapist's income."

"When my business started to take off, one of the first things I did was to pay my therapist his full fee. It feels good to be able to pay my own way."

"When I lost my job I was in despair, not only because I didn't have any income, but because when I needed it the most, I couldn't afford therapy. I was incredibly relieved when my therapist offered to lower his fee."

"I want to be extra good because I am on a reduced fee."

◆

VACATIONS

Many useful hours in therapy have been spent understanding a client's reactions to his or her therapist's vacations. Understanding your response to your therapist's vacation can provide an opportunity to learn about your feelings about separations. Many therapists provide coverage for clients during their absence; if you like, ask your therapist to recommend someone else to see during his or her vacation.

I react to my therapist's vacations with (circle any that apply): (sadness) (relief) (indifference) (anger) (jealousy) (panic) (mild anxiety) (eagerness) (depression).

◆

"Two weeks before my therapist's August vacation, things always seem to get worse. I start feeling depressed and afraid that I won't be able to make it without him. Then, lo and behold, once his vacation is in full swing, I do just fine."

"I like trying out my wings when my therapist is away."

"Sandy pointed out that each time she schedules a vacation, I miss the session right before. She wondered if I am showing her what it feels like to be left."

◆ Special Ground Rules for ◆ Group, Couple, and Family Therapy

Therapy becomes more complicated when more people participate in sessions. If you are in group, couple, or family therapy, the ground rules become more complex as they take everyone's needs into account. Here are some general guidelines.

BEGINNING AND LEAVING THERAPY

Because it often takes longer to become accustomed to a group than to individual therapy, many group therapists require that clients beginning a group stay for a specific trial period. It is also usual to require notice when a client is leaving. The client along with other group members can use this time to discuss the leave-taking and say goodbye.

CONFIDENTIALITY

It is essential that what you say or do remains in therapy so that you can feel free to reveal yourself. Just as your therapist must not reveal what he or she learns about you, anything you learn about others in therapy is to be kept confidential.

SOCIALIZING

Some therapists think that friendships outside the group session can make the job of therapy more complicated, because members may form coalitions or cliques and do the work of the group outside the session or keep secrets from the leader or other members.

Other therapists believe that the support group members can get from one another through friendships outweighs potential complications. All therapists recommend that group members bring issues or conflicts that arise during outside contacts into group therapy for discussion.

Sexual involvement between group members is most often thought to be inadvisable and potentially damaging to therapy. A group is a special protected place where intense feelings may be stirred up between group members. Learning that it is possible to have a range of feelings that can be talked about rather than acted upon is often one of the benefits of group therapy. Making the discussion of feelings of sexual attraction a part of the therapy may be uncomfortable at first but can lead to valuable discoveries.

My questions about the ground rules for my group, couple, or family therapy are

Now that you have had a chance to think about the etiquette of psychotherapy, you may have questions and reactions that you can share with your therapist and make grist for the mill of your own therapy.

·7·

Continuing the Journey

TASKS

1. Explore Your Reactions to Therapy
2. Deepen Your Therapeutic Relationship
3. Manage the Hard Times
4. Overcome the Obstacles to Change
5. Acknowledge Your Gains

How do you know when you've begun the middle phase of therapy? Generally, psychotherapists think of this phase as the time when you have learned what to do in therapy, have developed a solid working relationship with your therapist, and have made a commitment to see the work through. The middle phase can last anywhere from a few months to a number of years.

During the middle phase of your therapy, you may be delighted yet troubled by what you discover. You may experience periods of calm and periods of turmoil, periods of inactivity and periods of consolidation; you may wonder at times if you have lost your way.

This chapter contains a series of tasks to help you stay in touch with what you think and feel about therapy, strengthen your relationship with your therapist, manage the hard times along the way, acknowledge your progress, and overcome what gets in the way of changing. The next chapter will help you use your time between sessions to integrate what you are learning and keep your therapy on course. The seven tasks in these two chapters can be done in any order and can be returned to as needed during your therapy.

◆ Task 1 ◆
Explore Your Reactions
to Therapy

In Chapter 5, "Getting Off to a Good Start," you looked at your style of beginning. Now that you are in the midst of therapy, take time to consider what this phase is like for you. Begin by checking any of the following statements that apply to you.

Now that I am in the middle of therapy, I
_____ am working hard.
_____ feel that I have lost my way.
_____ am surprised by how much I am getting out of therapy.
_____ made a commitment and will persevere.
_____ am bored and wonder what else I might try or who else I could see in therapy.
_____ got off to a good start, but now I'm stalled.
_____ worry that I am not a good enough client.
_____ have confidence that all will work out and am working well in therapy.
_____ feel discouraged and think about giving up.
_____ am more involved in therapy than ever before.
_____ or, _____

This is (different from) (similar to) what usually happens when I am involved in the middle of an activity or relationship because

◆

"My therapy, like my life, has been a study in contrasts. At times I seem to be doing such intense work that every day brings increased understanding, some new response to an old situation, and so many powerful feelings that I can barely catch my breath. At other times, nothing seems to be going on at all. Then all of a sudden, wham, I am back into something important again."

"Once I'm through the initial excitement and challenge in a new situation, I feel trapped, and my couples' therapy is no exception. My therapist seems to be pleased that I'm talking about how restless I am in therapy, because he thinks my trapped feeling is a big part of my problem in my relationship."

◆ Task 2 ◆
Deepen Your Therapeutic Relationship

Although it was important for you and your therapist to establish a good working relationship at the beginning, neither of you can afford to rest on that achievement now. As in any good partnership, your therapy relationship requires continuing effort to keep it creative and alive.

Your part in deepening your relationship with your therapist consists of developing the skills that you learned in the beginning phase of your therapy:

- Let yourself be known.
- Listen to what is said.
- Ask questions.
- Attend to what you want from your therapist.
- Give your therapist feedback.

In addition, two new areas are involved in relationship building during this phase of therapy:

- Deal with issues of intimacy and autonomy.
- Make your thoughts and your feelings about your therapist a part of your therapy.

Deal with Issues of Intimacy and Autonomy

The two central tasks of any intimate relationship are staying close while maintaining a sense of autonomy and separateness. People often believe that they must sacrifice one or the other in order to be in a relationship. One person in a relationship may push for closeness, while the other pulls away in order to maintain some distance. This struggle can come up with your therapist. Your relationship with your therapist can be a laboratory where you can experiment with new ways of relating.

Now, in the middle of therapy, you are probably experiencing your therapist as an ally working on your behalf. You may feel grateful for the understanding he or she offers and the relief that you have begun to feel. Focusing on intimate parts of your life may result in a sense of closeness that you may not have expected in a professional relationship. You may find yourself feeling safe and trusting your therapist.

However, learning to trust another person can be a challenge, especially when you are vulnerable. You may discover that you feel close to your therapist at times and distant and wary at others. You may be worried about becoming too dependent or losing your own perspective.

The following statements represent a variety of responses to the ongoing process of building intimacy and autonomy with a therapist. You can return to this section at different points during your therapy to note how your responses change. Check any statements that resonate for you.

How do I deal with issues of closeness and separateness with my therapist?

_____ I hate it when my therapist and I see things differently.

_____ I trust my therapist.

_____ I'm scared to tell my therapist that he or she is mistaken about something.

_____ I know that my therapist is still on my side, even when we differ.

_____ I worry that my therapist has too much influence over me.

_____ I can depend on my therapist.

_____ I'm alienated from my therapist.

_____ I'm uncomfortable with how much I need my therapist.

_____ I listen to what my therapist has to say and make up my own mind.

_____ I feel wary of my therapist.

_____ I can disagree with my therapist.

_____ I'm afraid I'll get too dependent on my therapist, so I keep my distance.

_____ or, _____

I feel closest to my therapist when

I'm most likely to push my therapist away when

◆

"I thought the idea of therapy was to be totally honest and open. I was trying hard, but felt anxious a lot. When George told me that I didn't have to tell him every single thing about myself, I felt much better. He was not looking for forced confessions. I can keep some things to myself."

"There must be a way to be close to my therapist without feeling like I'm a vacuum cleaner, sucking up every bit of attention and caring I can get."

"I was hysterical, pacing around my therapist's office screaming about my impossible boss. In the middle of all this, I paused and said, 'No one but my mother has ever seen me like this.' I could feel how safe my therapy had become. During the next couple of sessions I was quiet and distant. Finally we figured out that I was humiliated that my therapist saw me so out of control. It opened up a whole new area to look at."

◆

Make Your Thoughts and Feelings About Your Therapist a Part of Your Therapy

By now you may be comfortable talking with your therapist about your reactions to other important people in your life but still hesitate to let your therapist know how you are responding to him or her. It can be difficult at first to be open about feelings of longing, disappointment, or anger, especially if you have had little practice in doing so outside therapy. You may believe that your reactions are irrelevant, be embarrassed by the intensity of your feelings, or think that you have more important matters to talk about. You may wonder why it would be useful for you to bring your reactions to your therapist into your therapy.

As in any relationship, some of your reactions to your therapist will be based on the realities of the current situation and some will be colored by your past experiences. Many therapists believe that we misunderstand or overreact to present events because of unresolved past issues. These therapists expect that from time to time we will have reactions toward them that have more to do with these unresolved issues than with what is happening in the here and now. Your therapist may help you to sort out your "transference" reactions, "script issues," or "unfinished business," or simply to discuss the current realities of your professional relationship. Therapy can provide a safe place for us to experience, understand, and resolve the sort of difficult reactions that hamper our personal relationships.

Use the next exercise to explore your responses to your therapist and see which portion is related to the here and now and which is related to your past.

I had a dramatic, intense, or seemingly inappropriate reaction to my therapist when

This reminds me of reactions to

◆

"Dr. H says that I find fault and argue with him. Last week he pointed out how my father and I were afraid to be close to each other and would fight to be in contact with each other. I feel closer to my therapist now."

"Having vivid sexual fantasies about my therapist is embarrassing, especially since he's old enough to be my grandfather. It's like a

real crush combined with a deep longing. I even started dressing up for sessions. When I finally got up the nerve to tell him what was happening, it was such a relief."

"When someone sounds mad, I freak out. My mom got violent when she lost her temper. In group, when I start panicking, the leader has me talk to the person I'm scared of and, then, to imagine that my mom is sitting right there and to pretend to talk to her. It helps me get the differences between then and now straight."

"I'm getting tired of my therapist relating everything that happens during our sessions to my feelings about her. If I'm late, I'm trying to avoid her. If I'm quiet, I'm hiding from her. She's off the mark; I have other things going on in my life besides how I respond to her."

"I'm having lots of strong feelings about my therapist, but he doesn't seem to want to listen to what I have to say. I don't know what to do."

◆ Task 3 ◆
Manage the Hard Times

You may find times when the going gets rough and it is difficult to continue your journey. What causes hard times in therapy? In general, facing painful discoveries, managing strong feelings, dealing with conflicts and misunderstandings, and experiencing the frustration of no change in sight are the central difficulties clients face. But being aware of what you find particularly difficult about therapy can help you anticipate and deal with your hard times.

It is during hard times in therapy that your therapist's knowledge and skill are especially important. With his or her help, you can transform roadblocks into occasions for learning. It is also during these times that you need courage and patience to continue on the course that you have set for yourself.

I am finding therapy particularly difficult now because

Facing Painful Discoveries

Recalling emotionally charged childhood memories or facing realities about ourselves, our loved ones, and our life can cause pain. You may discover aspects of yourself that you do not like. You may begin to see some of the people around you in a different, disappointing, or more realistic light.

The more we allow the painful feelings or events in our life to enter our consciousness, the more control we have over what we do with them. When you bring painful feelings or events into therapy, you also make it possible for your therapist to offer some perspective and encouragement.

It has been painful for me to discover . . . about myself

It has been painful to discover . . . about people I care about

It has been painful to discover . . . about my past

It has been painful to discover . . . about my current life

Many clients find that the following discoveries are difficult to accept. Check any statements that seem to apply to you.

_____ I see the part I play in my problems with people.
_____ I long for someone to take care of me.

_____ I have chosen friends or mates who are bound to let me down.
_____ My childhood is over and I will never get what I needed then.
_____ I hide my feelings behind a facade.
_____ I understand why I do things, but I'm still repeating the same old patterns.
_____ I will probably be in therapy a long time; my problems are more complicated than I thought.
_____ I am not sure that I really want to change.
_____ I have idealized or undervalued my parents.
_____ I take responsibility for the mistakes of people I love.
_____ I will never get my parents' approval.
_____ Someone I trusted has hurt me.
_____ I do things to get even with people.
_____ I am competitive.
_____ I am envious.
_____ I provoke others.
_____ I don't like myself very much.
_____ or, _____

◆

"People in my therapy group finally convinced me that I get depressed when I give to everyone else and neglect myself. When I try to figure out what I want, I draw a blank. All of my decisions —what to eat and wear, what job to take—were based on what I imagined would please other people. I have no idea how to decide anything anymore."

"After I told my therapist about my recurring childhood dream about a horse wetting me with his soft nose, she became convinced that my father, who had sexually molested other kids, had done some sexual stuff with me. I'm so confused and depressed. I loved my father so."

"My therapist has begun massaging my jaws where I have chronic tension and pain. Suddenly, as my jaw is relaxing, I am beginning to remember how I would grit my teeth when my parents, whom I have always remembered as being loving and kind, would insult or criticize me. It's a whole new way to see them, and I feel sad about losing the idea that my parents were perfect."

"My supervisor reprimanded me for writing what she termed a hostile letter. That night I dreamed that I was out running and my pants were falling down, exposing my bottom. I couldn't shake the feeling of humiliation. My therapist helped me see how I felt exposed by my supervisor."

◆

Coping with Strong Feelings

Therapy can provide a safe place where the full range of our feelings is accepted and where we learn how to talk about what we feel. Sometimes it is hard work to manage the strong and unexpected emotions that come up.

Complete those sentences that resonate for you.

I am feeling vulnerable now because

It is difficult for me to manage my feelings during therapy sessions when

It has been hard to cope with my feelings in between sessions when

◆

"When my therapist pointed out that I was reacting to my daughter as though she were my depriving mother, I felt incredibly guilty and depressed. What a miserable person I am to treat my daughter so badly. Gradually, I took in that my therapist did not share my point of view, did not see me as a horrible person."

"Therapy has been helping me to see what a pushover I am in every area of my life. I've begun to flex my muscles at work, and

sometimes I go too far. Anticipating that my boss or co-workers may step on my toes, I am edgy and ready to pounce."

"The analysis is starting to scare me. I feel like I have the aware-ness of an amoeba, the backbone of a jellyfish, and the defenses of an armadillo with nothing inside."

"I used to feel pretty numb. Now that I am doing body work, boy, do I feel plenty—mostly sadness. I burst into tears on the street, during meetings at work, while I'm watching TV. Even though my therapist assures me that this is a temporary state, I'm scared that I've lost control."

◆

Resolving Disagreements, Misunderstandings, and Conflicts

From time to time you may find yourself having differences with your therapist or others who are part of your therapy. Even when you know that differences are an inevitable part of human interaction, these conflicts can be painful when they occur. Keep in mind that resolving discord often brings about a new level of closeness and understanding between the people involved. In therapy, periods of turmoil are often followed by movement.

Complete any of the sentences that describe your experience. In-clude a description of how you handled your difficulties with the others involved.

It seemed that my (therapist) (group member) (partner) (family member) was insensitive to me when

I felt hurt or angry when my (therapist) (group member) (partner) (family member)

I think that my (therapist) (group member) (partner) (family member) judged me when

I need to talk with _____ about

◆

"I told Dominick that he had been thoughtless because he laughed when I described my problems with my son. He agreed. Then he said that sometimes he was clumsy and insensitive, and that he was sorry. I was caught off guard. I had expected a big hassle about why I was so upset; instead I felt really cared for."

"My group kept getting on my case for taking care of my wife after one of her drunks. They just didn't know how hard it would be to leave her on the floor for the kids to see. I finally blew my stack at them and someone in group suggested that I go to a self-help group for families of alcoholics in addition to group, and that's helped a lot."

"Now that my mother is sick, I keep feeling my therapist, Paul, thinks that I'm a bad daughter because I don't have more to do with her. He keeps asking me how she is doing and if I've seen her. He seems to care more about her than about me."

◆

Continuing When No Change Is in Sight

You may feel disheartened when change does not come easily or quickly; when well-considered plans go awry; when deeply desired new behavior seems beyond reach; and when painful emotions recur.

It is hard to appreciate that therapy is a *process*, which does not follow a straight path. You may take three steps forward and two steps back. Your relationship with your therapist, your patience, and your knowledge of what makes change difficult will help see you through.

◆

"I get so sick and tired of the same old issues. I am tired of how hard I am on myself, tired of this major voice of criticism in my head. I wish I would just stop it already."

"I'm learning in therapy how I am attracted to women who are intrusive and controlling, just like my mother. Dr. B. said that as I become aware of this pattern I will resolve it. In the meantime, what do I do? I want a good relationship now."

"I really thought that I had gotten over being so angry with my mother. Now I'm feeling all those old feelings again. I'm right back where I started, and I feel so discouraged."

◆ Task 4 ◆
Overcome the Obstacles to Change

Although explanations vary as to why we stumble on the path to change, most schools of therapy concur that the following obstacles create problems for even the most willing client:

- Outmoded childhood solutions
- Self-defeating beliefs
- Self-defeating behavior
- Lack of support

Identifying and understanding what is getting in the way of making the changes you want is an important step in the change process. Overcoming these barriers may bring unexpected benefits because they may be interfering with your life outside therapy as well.

Outmoded Childhood Solutions

Ironically, some of the solutions that got us through the difficult times of our childhood are often obstacles to getting what we want as adults. We learned to do what we believed would work in our original families. Our patterns of coping worked well enough to get us through our childhood but may not work well for us now. Often these patterns are self-defeating rather than self-enhancing.

These patterns change gradually as we begin to notice and name them and as we learn that we no longer need them. Realizing that we have many resources now that we lacked as children and that our current world is different from the world of our childhood can give us the strength to leave the old patterns behind. Furthermore, becoming aware of the part of us that wishes to stay with what we know rather than risk change can help us make real choices about what we want to do now.

These are examples of outmoded childhood solutions that others identified and changed during their therapy:

◆

"My mother's motto was 'If you can't say something nice, don't say anything at all.' I wanted to be a good girl more than anything else when I was a kid, so I used to avoid conflict at all costs. I'm beginning to see that I can voice a strong opinion and even get mad, and people will stick around and deal with me."

"My dad was an alcoholic, and my brother and I never knew what was coming next. One minute he'd be real sweet and make up to us, and the next he'd be a mean bastard. I had to be on my toes all the time to make sure we didn't get hurt. Now I'm suspicious of anyone in authority."

"It was so chaotic at home when I was growing up that I taught myself to detach from what was going on around me; it made it possible to survive in the midst of all the noise and mess. The trouble is that my detachment has become automatic. It gets in the way when I want to get close to someone."

"Life was not easy with seven brothers and with my mother in and out of mental hospitals. I learned to get whatever I needed from school, neighbors, and any outside activity I could find. My two ex-wives said that I always had one foot out the door. I want this marriage to succeed. In couples' therapy, I am working on keeping both feet in the relationship."

"I still remember my mother sitting on her bed crying for hours after her miscarriage. I was so scared. I decided to keep everything in order, whether it was my toys, my feelings, or my relationships. If I let anything get out of order, everything will come tumbling down."

◆

As therapy encourages you to question the outmoded solutions in your life, you may worry that you will be lost or disoriented without them. Although change will eventually create new freedom, you may need to appreciate what you are giving up before you arrive at a comfortable new balance in your life. Recognizing how useful your old solutions were in the past will help you to say goodbye to what you no longer need now.

This exercise will help you to learn more about your own outmoded solutions and help you to explore your thoughts and feelings about changing.

As you engage in the next exercises, think about an outmoded solution or problem that you would like to change. Focus on your feelings about changing it.

I want to change _____ **because**

In the past, this solution may have helped me to

I am hesitant to change because

◆

"When I realized that my way of making everything in my life magical and filled with possibility was disappearing, I felt a

tremendous sense of loss. Before, everything I did had been supercharged with excitement. Now, even though I am more in charge of what happens to me, I feel like a regular person living a regular life."

◆

Self-defeating Beliefs

Has therapy helped you to see that you hold certain mistaken assumptions that color your perspective and affect your behavior? You may find that you evaluate yourself and others through a filter of unfounded, outdated, or distorted beliefs.

As children, we form our ideas about ourselves and others based on our limited, childlike perceptions and reasoning and often accept without second thought what the grownups around us believe. While we may update our beliefs as we have more experience, some of our assumptions persist, unexamined, into our adult life. We may not even be aware of the full impact they have on us until we look at them closely.

Take the time to review some of the assumptions you make that may be standing in the way of your growth. Check any of the statements that reflect your beliefs.

_____ A person who really cares about me should know what I want.

_____ If I were a strong person, I would not feel sad, anxious, or mad.

_____ It's wrong to burden others with my problems.

_____ If I were a better person, I wouldn't be having problems.

_____ I shouldn't feel angry at my (kids) (mother) (father) (mate) (friends) (co-worker) (boss).

_____ Parents are to blame if children have problems.

_____ If I work at it, I can decide what feelings to feel.

_____ Everyone will love me if I'm really good.

_____ If I feel too pleased with myself, I'll become arrogant.

_____ I shouldn't have to ask anyone for help.

_____ It's wrong to put myself first.

_____ Perfection is achievable with hard work.

_____ I should always say what I feel.

_____ It's important to stay in control of your feelings at all times.

_____ People need to be told when they are wrong.

_____ I shouldn't disagree with my (boss) (parent) (mate) (teacher) (friend).

_____ No one else has problems like mine.

_____ I can't really trust anyone.

_____ or, _____

As you think about the assumptions you hold, you may see how your beliefs lead you to continue with self-defeating behavior or out-moded solutions to your problems. For example, if you assume that it's wrong to put yourself first, you may care for others in the hope that they will take care of you without your making your needs clear.

◆

"Even though I know that my perfectionism sets me up for dis-appointment, I'm scared that I'll never do a lick of work again if I stop pushing myself hard."

"I never told anyone that I was a straight-A student in college. Each time I'd see my grades posted on the bulletin board, I'd be thrilled. I was lonely and wanted to share my happiness with someone, but I'd been taught that pride was a sin."

"My group keeps telling me to let my wife know what I want. What's the point? If she really loved me, she would want to do things for me without my having to ask."

◆

Self-defeating Behavior

There are things we do that are too gratifying or exciting to give up easily. Even when we understand that we pay a high price in the long run, we may resist changing. The immediate gratification of overeating, losing our temper, or having one more drink seems to be hard to resist. Some of us develop a pattern of impulsive action that undermines our positive sense of ourselves, causes pain, or makes relationships fragile and unsatisfying. In some instances, when this behavior leads to sub-stance abuse or serious self-neglect, it is dangerous and damaging.

We can also get rewards from others for behavior that is difficult or self-defeating. We may attract more attention for making or being in trouble than for doing well. These secondary benefits can make it hard to relinquish even the most painful problems.

◆

"I'm starting to see that if I stop acting like a waif, I'm going to get less attention from my family and friends."

"When I get angry, I like to get it right off my chest. I'm not going to be the one with the ulcer. I know I hurt people's feelings, but I wouldn't be honest if I didn't say what I'm feeling."

"My father is self-involved and lives through me. He wants me to be a great academic, and he took so much credit for my success in high school that I hardly mattered. Now I've been doing poorly in college. I am learning in therapy that I don't want to give my father the satisfaction of my achieving. The revenge is sweet, but it is my life that is suffering."

"When my husband neglects me, I start a flirtation and sometimes an affair. Even though I can see the pain that this has caused and part of me wants to stop, part of me doesn't."

◆

Continue to think about a self-defeating pattern or a current problem as you answer the following.

Although I want to change, _____ I may have to give up

If I give this up, I may miss

Lack of Support

You may be finding it difficult to change because the people in your life are not supporting your efforts. The most loving friends and family members may not know how to help you change.

Some may be threatened or thrown off balance by a new you; they may want the old you back, whatever the cost. Others feel close to you because of the very pattern you are trying to change: because you never express anger, you are the caretaker in the relationship, or the life of the party. Still others may be jealous of your success.

You can use therapy to help you get more support for the changes you want to make. Your therapist may suggest ways for you to ask people specifically for what you want, suggest how you can give accurate feedback to the people who are not supportive, or help you learn to tolerate changing without the support of your loved ones.

It may also be that your workplace, community, or society at large fails to support your growth. Some therapists make the impact of your community or culture an important part of therapy and encourage political or social action. They believe that it is therapeutic to help clients to experience their personal power and be involved in efforts to change those conditions that limit personal growth. Others believe that this broader focus does not belong in the province of therapy. This distinction is not based upon the therapist's approach; feminist therapists, for example, can be found in all schools of therapy.

If your therapist does not bring a broader social perspective to your therapy, you may want to supplement your work with reading and activity in groups that do have this focus. (See "Resources" for suggested readings and contacts.)

◆

"I want to be a good Catholic and feel good about being gay at the same time."

"Sometimes I think my husband liked me better when I was depressed. Now that I am asking him to help out and letting him know that I don't like it when he stays out late, he says I'm a bitch. My therapist suggested that we do some work as a couple to get us over this hump."

"Now that I feel ready for a more responsible job, I can see that women do not stand a ghost of a chance in my company."

"My psychiatrist says that my mother was an alcoholic and I should consider going to a group especially for adult children of

alcoholics. If anyone in my family found out, they would disown me. It's like we all have an unspoken agreement not to say that Mom was a drunk."

"I guess I'll just have to live with my mother's disapproval. She can't seem to get past the fact that I am a lesbian and won't be having the life that made her happy. It doesn't seem to matter to her that Cathy and I have a loving relationship and I've never felt better."

◆

How are the people in your life supporting the changes that you are making?

Who has not offered as much support as you would like?

What kind of support would you like?

Who else can you reach out to for support?

◆ Task 5 ◆
Acknowledge Your Gains

Although there are hard times in therapy, there are good times as well. As you continue in therapy, you will notice that you are beginning to make changes, some small and some significant. You may feel strong, unexpected emotions, come to terms with your past, and develop new problem-solving skills. Giving yourself credit along the way helps you build on your progress and sustain you during the hard times.

Can you identify turning points in your therapy? You may have developed a new awareness or experienced the powerful sense of recognition and understanding that many therapists call insight. Perhaps you have recovered a childhood memory or clarified a central issue. It is satisfying to both therapist and client to recognize how everything fits together. You may be moved to tears or laughter by the excitement of making sense of an obscure or troubling issue.

Have you experienced emotions that were unavailable to you before, feeling joy at being alive or rage at a neglectful parent? You may have behaved in a way that you did not dream was possible, saying no to something you did not want or allowing yourself to feel cared for and accepted.

A turning point in therapy is a marker that signifies how far you've come. Recognizing turning points helps sustain you during difficult times and shows that there is light at the end of the tunnel.

What have been your turning points in therapy? Complete those statements that remind you of discoveries or experiences you found particularly powerful or meaningful.

I saw things in a new way when

It was a powerful experience when

For the first time I

♦

"Analysis has freed me from the tyranny of bad thoughts and feelings. I remember very clearly the day I finally reached the point where I had told my analyst all the things I had never told anyone else: all the things I had done that I was ashamed of, all the things I thought I was ashamed of. I felt a tremendous sense of relief on that day, as though I had been released from prison. In a sense I had."

"For the first time I realized in my gut that I could say no. I was no longer that dazed eleven-year-old girl with her drunken daddy. I was truly a grown-up woman with choices."

"Therapy helped me see how my parents' experience in the Holocaust profoundly affected me. I was their hope that they would never again be faced with unhappiness. To suggest that I felt pained would be cruel to them. So I hid. I told no one what I felt unless it was cheerful. I told no one what I thought unless it was optimistic. My aim was to be perfect."

"I used to dream that I was anxious and alone, lost in the subways. Last night I was calm and pleased as I dreamed that I had been put in charge of redesigning the subway system. I realized how the dark underground part of me, my dark desires and hidden fantasies, no longer terrify me. I am in charge now."

"When my therapist massaged my neck to release the tight bands that seem to constrict me, I reexperienced sitting at the kitchen table for hours while my dictatorial father went through a litany of criticism. As I recalled that scene, I began to feel the power to say no. No, I won't sit at that table and take abuse, and no, I won't sit still and be manipulated by my lover now."

◆

Be sure to take the time to give yourself credit for your gains.

I recognize that I am changing because

It is getting easier for me to

I no longer feel

I am changing my beliefs about

◆

"For the first time since I was a teenager, I visited my parents and we did not fight. Maybe next time, I'll even relax and enjoy myself."

"I have come to accept and even feel proud of being gay. Now I'm ready to find a lover with whom I can share my life."

"I enjoy spending time alone with my wife now. It used to be that we were always on the go or with other people. We even took a friend on our honeymoon. We are beginning to get to know each other for the first time."

"Watch out, world—I've got a big mouth now."

◆

•8•
Making Your Therapy Work

TASKS

1. Use the Tools for Success in Therapy
2. Keep Your Therapy Moving

You have a central role in making your therapy work. Since you spend a limited amount of time in therapy, your continuing activity and awareness between sessions can affect how well and how quickly you progress.

The first task teaches you how to apply some of the tools used in your sessions. Learning these tools for yourself can help you integrate what you are learning while extending and deepening the impact of your therapy. Over time, as your therapist demonstrates how he or she uses the tools with you, you will master them, gradually learning to become your own therapist. Return to this section anytime that you need to review how to make them your own.

The second task will be helpful if your therapy seems to be drifting or stalled. You can use the guidelines to revitalize your therapy and to keep things on course.

◆ Task 1 ◆
Use the Tools for Success in Therapy

The same five tools that you have been developing and strengthening during your therapy can be employed to help you in your life as well. These tools build on skills that you already have and require only some forethought and practice to use them well.

- Curiosity
- Powers of observation
- Empathy
- Receptivity
- Clear communication

Practice using these tools to work on something that is currently on your mind: an issue that you and your therapist are discussing; a problem that is preoccupying you; an interpretation that inspires or puzzles you; an interpretation that makes sense to you intellectually but doesn't move you emotionally; an obstacle to change that you identified in the last chapter.

◆

"My therapist tells me I must be doing something to make my boss so angry; it happens with all my bosses."

"I don't know what to talk about in therapy."

"I've been so anxious lately. I can't figure out why."

"It happened again last night in group. I was just trying to be helpful and they thought I was getting off on being superior. It must be true, but I don't really get it."

◆

The (problems) (issues) (concerns) I would like to focus on are

As you learn about the tools for success and respond to the questions on the next few pages, think about the problems you have identified. You will notice that these tools work together in overlapping cycles. As you employ one tool with increasing success, you may find changes in how you employ the other tools as well.

Curiosity

Curiosity is an inquiring, searching attitude that prompts us to be interested in and to ask questions about ourselves and the world around us. The answers we get can help dispel ignorance and confusion and make sense out of our feelings, thoughts, and experiences. In addition, recapturing our childlike sense of wonder makes life more exciting.

Think of yourself as a detective searching for clues about something that is on your mind. Here are some questions that may apply:

How did this happen?
Why did I act that way?
How did I get myself in this situation?
Why am I bothered about this now?
What made me react this way?
What would _____ do in this situation?
When did this begin?
What might my therapist say about this?
What does this person / situation / feeling remind me of?
What are my options?
Where and under what conditions have I done this before?
How would I like things to be different?

Now complete these sentences.

When I think about my problem, I wonder about

When my therapist, group members, or friends address this issue, they wonder about

If I were helping a friend deal with this issue, I would wonder about

As you formulate your questions, you may find that you have more work to do gathering information before you can hope to answer them. That's where some of the other tools can be useful—your powers of observation, your receptivity, and your ability to communicate clearly.

◆

"My therapist asks me questions about my childhood and I just can't remember much. So I started asking my parents, my aunt, and my grandmother about what life was like when I was a kid. I learned so much about what they were like and what it must have been like for me. It was fun for all of us."

"My mother got silent when I asked about how my grandfather died. Pretty soon I figured out that there were some things that you just couldn't ask about. In my group I am learning that I can get answers."

◆

Powers of Observation

You can gather the information needed to resolve your issues by noticing what happens within and around you. Continue your investigation by focusing on your inner life: your thoughts, fantasies and dreams, feelings and sensations. All of these offer clues about what is going on and how you can make things different. Observing what is happening around you will also help you to understand if this is a recurrent issue or follows a pattern. You may choose to follow up on the problem you were focusing on in the previous section or on a different issue.

Think back to the last time you remember having the problem that you are considering. Imagine that you are actually back in the situation as the problem is occurring. Give yourself time to put yourself in the picture and experience what was happening then. Now answer the following questions from the perspective of how you felt then.

As I focus on my body, I notice that I am experiencing (Is there a tightness in your chest? Are there aches in your head, neck, or shoulders? Is your heart pounding, your respiration shallow or deep, slow or rapid? Are you holding your breath?)

I am feeling (Are feelings of anger, fear, sadness, or pleasure being stirred up by what is happening? Do your feelings change?)

I am thinking and doing (Describe the sequence of what happened and your thinking during the time. If other people are involved, describe what they are doing also.)

What happened right before the problem appeared and what happened right afterward?

It may be useful to understand if this is a recurrent issue or follows a pattern.

This time, you are going to move back gradually through time. Think back to your life five years ago. Can you remember having the same feelings or being in a similar situation at that time? Recall your life ten years ago. Did you experience the same issue at that time? Continue back through your life to the very first time that you remember a similar feeling or found yourself in the same quandary.

As I went back through time, I noticed

Review the dreams that you have written in your journal to see if any of them reminds you of this issue. If your problem has occurred recently, see if you can recall any dreams that you have had in the last two weeks. Think about your dream and use your journal or a separate piece of paper as you complete the next sentences.

The characters and specific images of my dream remind me of

My feelings about the dream are

As I read the dream, I notice these themes

Now let your mind focus in on the issues that concern you. For ten to twenty minutes, allow yourself to write anything and everything that occurs to you—whatever comes up without regard for logic or order, even if it seems trivial or is embarrassing or impolite.

Let some time pass before you return to what you have written.

As I reread what I have written, I realize

◆

"As I talk to my boss, I start to have trouble talking because my throat is so tight. I can just hear my therapist asking what might be sticking in my throat. It is the anger that I don't dare express to him; I'm choking on rage."

"As I imagined back to other times when I was panicked the way I am now on the subway, I remembered being in the car with my dad, who had been drinking and was driving much too fast. I was terrified, but everyone ignored me. My parents were busy fighting, my brother thought it was funny because I was crying."

"I spent last week tortured by depression, hating myself. When my therapist asked me what happened right before I started getting depressed, I remembered that my husband didn't come through for me on something that he promised. My therapist looked at me with a spark of recognition and reminded me that instead of getting angry, I get depressed."

"The young boys who keep appearing in my dreams are reminders that I am ignoring the boyish side of myself, the part of me that is fun-loving and mischievous."

◆

Empathy

Empathy is the ability to put ourselves in another's place in order to experience what he or she is feeling or thinking. All of us want to be known and understood; this kind of sensitivity is a great gift.

Understanding the feelings and motives of others encourages us to be more tolerant. It can help us find acceptable compromises. Using empathy with ourselves helps us to be more self-accepting and less self-critical.

Does a current problem involve someone else? If so, use the next exercise to practice understanding his or her point of view. If several people are involved, you may want to repeat the exercise from each perspective.

What thoughts and feelings might _____
have about this issue?

How would he or she see my part in the problem?

Using the tools of empathy with yourself will enable you to use other tools for success in therapy more effectively. If you are not giving yourself a hard time about a problem, you can be free to be curious and observant.

To practice being more self-accepting and less self-critical, leave behind your imaginary role as a detective and pretend you are a benevolent friend (see page 18). Choose a problem or issue about which you are particularly self-critical.

What might _____ think about my problem?

Knowing about my problem, how would he or she feel toward me?

What might he or she say to me about this issue?

Another way to extend your empathy to yourself is to pretend this problem belongs to someone about whom you care deeply. Draw on the empathy you have for this person.

How I would view this problem if it belonged to someone else? (Be generous!)

◆

"In times of hopelessness or anxiety, I think about how Lila might approach my distress. She is understanding and accepting and doesn't feel that I am worthless. Just that knowledge makes me feel better."

"I feel for my husband when he tells how much he misses the good times we used to have. I had dragged him to couples' therapy because I didn't think he really cared all that much. Now I see that he's withdrawn out of disappointment."

◆

Receptivity

Staying open to new ideas can be difficult, but it is vital if we want to continue changing and growing. Especially during hard times, others may be able to provide a new perspective on problems that seem impossible to resolve on our own.

Give thoughtful consideration to what others suggest, even if it flies in the face of everything you heard while growing up or anything you've always believed. In addition to therapy, we can learn from books, classes, or our own family and friends. Being receptive does not mean that we adopt ideas indiscriminately; it means that we give them a thorough hearing.

What does my (therapist) (group) (friend) (family member) think about this problem?

What seems relevant to me about what they think?

I am finding it hard to accept

However, I have learned

◆

"It took maybe twenty-five confrontations before I could believe that I was behaving in an angry way when I teased Bonnie in group."

"When my supervisor said that I am critical and set impossibly high standards for my employees, I was angry and offended. He just wasn't understanding how the people who work for me take advantage of my generosity and slack off. That evening his words played over and over again in my head. I felt calmer and realized he's right."

◆

Clear Communication

Therapy encourages you, even teaches you, how to talk about your thoughts and feelings as clearly as possible. Being able to put your thoughts and feelings into words:

- Gives you a chance to understand yourself better.
- Increases the likelihood that you will be understood.
- Increases the likelihood of getting what you want.
- Gives you the time to consider and plan constructive action.

Pick an issue you are working on now that involves communicating with someone else. Is there something specific that you would like this other person to know, some feedback about his or her behavior, a feeling or thought that you hesitate to share? You may have a question that you want to ask.

I'm having a hard time expressing myself about

Now make a statement as though you were speaking to the other person.

I want you to know

Here's how you can increase the possibility that your listener will be receptive to what you are saying:

- Timing is important. Choose an appropriate time and place.
- Avoid attacking, judging, or blaming your listener.
- Own your own thoughts and feelings. Say "I am furious" rather than "You make me mad." Say "I imagined you were late because you didn't care enough" rather than "You don't care how I feel."
- Separate out your thoughts and beliefs from your feelings. The basic feelings are sad, mad, happy, or scared.

- Take responsibility for your part in any difficulty or miscommunication; this may help the other person to take responsibility too.

Look back to your completion of "I want you to know" and see if what you have written can be restated in a way that might make it more likely that you will be heard.

I want you to know

◆

"My therapist tells me that I keep saying 'the feeling' rather than 'I feel' and that I talk about having to do things as if I have no choice. I am beginning to see how the way I use words reflects my feeling of helplessness and makes me feel even more helpless."

"When I am most desperate for help, I look the most competent and untouchable. I get frightened and feel that I have to keep control and then become rigid and distant. I signal for people to stay away and then I wonder why no one takes care of me. I am learning that I need to let people know what it is that I need."

"No one in my family ever got angry. It just wasn't done. To have what I am experiencing labeled as anger or rage, to be able to describe the experiences to others, to put words to all that inchoate feeling—what a pleasure!"

◆

The exercises in this task gave you a sample of how to learn and practice the tools you acquire in therapy and broaden the work that you and your therapist do together. As your therapy continues, you will become even more adept in using these tools for yourself.

The experience of using the tools may lead you to some new questions or insights about problems, which you can bring back into your therapy. Events, feelings, or observations may be falling into place. You may have new ideas or see patterns that went unnoticed before. You may also have noted difficulties you have in being curious, employing your powers of observation, being empathic with yourself or someone else, being receptive to others, or communicating which you can discuss with your therapist.

The next task will give you the opportunity to apply what you have learned in your therapy and from this book to keep your therapy moving if you are bogged down.

◆ Task 2 ◆
Keep Your Therapy Moving

There are plateaus in therapy, quiet times when the intensity lessens and you consolidate your gains.

There are times when therapy can seem stale or boring. You are working on the same old things in the same old ways, or you don't know what to talk about. You're feeling restless, you wonder why so little is happening. If this is how it seems to you, describe your experience by completing the next statement.

I am feeling stuck in therapy because

Here are some suggestions about how to get moving again.

◆ *Talk to your therapist.* Have you let your therapist know that you are feeling stuck? If not, why are you hesitating? Turn to page 87 for some guidelines about how to give your therapist this important feedback.

I want my therapist to know that

What my therapist says about my feeling stuck is

• **Review your focus.**   Look back at your goals on page 90. Do they still seem relevant? Have you gotten off the track? Are you and your therapist in accord about where you are heading?

The issues that are important to me now are

• **Renew your therapeutic relationship.**   To stay vital and interesting, all relationships need special attention from time to time. Review your part in building a good working relationship. See page 83 to be sure that both of you are doing your parts in maintaining a good relationship.

In order to solidify our working relationship, I could

In order to solidify our working relationship, my therapist could

• **Notice if you are avoiding anything.**   Sometimes we feel stuck when we are avoiding a difficult or painful area. Turn to page 120 to see if you may be avoiding a hard time in therapy. You may be hesitant to go further because you are frightened of facing more painful material.

It would be difficult for me to face

• **Expand your therapy to include something new.**   You may be ready to deepen your therapy by trying something new. You could come to sessions more or less frequently; add group, individual, couple, or family therapy; keep a journal; bring your fantasies and dreams to therapy; try the couch, body work, a marathon group session. (See page

37 for more suggestions about how to think about what might expand your therapy.)

You and your therapist can discuss what the two of you might do that would change or add to your therapy.

I am interested in changing my therapy to include

• *Use the tools for success in therapy.* Using "I feel stuck in my therapy" as the issue on which to focus, you can return to Task 1 in this chapter to help you sort out what may be going on now. Begin by using the exercise on curiosity to formulate your questions, and then consider what you might observe about being stuck and how open you are to taking in information, especially from your therapist.

• *Evaluate your therapy.* If you have followed the relevant suggestions so far, and you are still puzzled or dissatisfied, a more formal evaluation is in order. The next chapter helps you think about your therapy.

• *See if you are ready to leave therapy.* Perhaps you feel stuck or have little to say because you are actually ready to end therapy. Turn to Chapter 10 to help you decide whether the time has come to say goodbye.

• *Do nothing.* Sometimes seeds that are planted take time to root and grow. If you are patient, time itself may take care of your being stuck.

·9·
Evaluating Your Therapy

TASKS

1. Review Your Reasons for Evaluating Your Therapy
2. Reflect on Your Working Relationship with Your Therapist
3. Sort Out Your Reactions to Therapy
4. Consider Your Therapist's Competence and Professional Behavior
5. Use a Consultation if Needed

Evaluating what is going well and what could be improved on in therapy helps to keep you active, aware, and involved on your own behalf. An evaluation can be useful in all phases of therapy: in the beginning if you are uncertain about the experience; in the middle to pinpoint areas that need attention; and at the end to help you decide when to leave.

Bring your ideas to your sessions and include your therapist in the evaluation process. Therapists want to know about their clients' needs. Together you can consider what is and is not working for you in therapy.

◆ Task 1 ◆
Review Your Reasons
for Evaluating Your Therapy

How is therapy going? You may be wondering how it could be improved. Something—you may not be sure just what—may not seem quite right. Or you may be clear about a problem and be unsure about what to do to resolve it. First, let's get down to specifics for clues about what is going on.

Why do you want to look more closely at your therapy right now? Check any of the following statements that reflect your responses.

_____ I think that I should be getting more from therapy.
_____ My therapist and I are not working well together.
_____ I seem to have lost my sense of direction.
_____ I am concerned about how competent my therapist is.
_____ I seem to be getting worse instead of better.
_____ My therapist doesn't seem to understand me.
_____ I dread going to my sessions.
_____ I have doubts about my therapist's ethics or competence.
_____ I keep thinking about quitting therapy.
_____ My therapy has become boring and predictable.
_____ I am in constant turmoil about my therapy.
_____ My therapist and I don't get along.
_____ or, _____

Are You Satisfied with Your Progress?

You may begin to doubt your therapy because you are unsure about whether or not you are making enough progress. It can be difficult to see how far you have come, particularly if you are having a hard time right now. (See page 120 to review why you may be having a hard time and page 148 if you are stuck.) To gain some perspective, look back over the entire course of your therapy. It may help if you review what you have written throughout this book.

Initially you may not see changes and yet your therapy may be working; understanding is an important first step. And sometimes you feel worse before you feel better.

When I think about the progress I have made since beginning therapy, I am pleased that I have been able to

I wish that I had made more progress in

Your Serious Problems Persist

If you began therapy with a serious difficulty or because you engaged in dangerous behavior, it is particularly important that your therapy is effective in helping you to change.

By the time you reach the middle phase of therapy, you should begin to experience some relief. If you check any of the following statements, something more *must* be done for you.

_____ I engage in violent behavior.

_____ I engage in suicidal behavior.

_____ I find myself in dangerous situations.

_____ I abuse drugs or alcohol.

_____ I am not functioning well enough to take care of myself or to work.

_____ I am extremely depressed.

_____ I am extremely anxious or panic-stricken.

_____ I see or hear things that others do not see and hear.

Some therapists are not prepared to deal with serious or dangerous difficulties. Either their training or their professional experience has not included these kinds of problems. If you are not gaining control over a serious difficulty, outpatient talk therapy may not be enough of a help.

Here are a few things to consider with your therapist or a consultant:

- Finding another therapist, skilled in your particular problem.
- Psychotropic medicine added to talk psychotherapy to help you control your dangerous behavior or serious symptom. (See page 34 to reacquaint yourself with the kinds of problems medication can alleviate.)
- A stay in an in-patient psychiatric hospital until you have sufficient control over the serious difficulty you are experiencing.

◆

"Suicide was constantly on my mind. I kept finding myself on the roof, inches from the edge. My parents insisted that I see another therapist for a consultation. The consultant said that I needed the protection of a hospital. I hated every minute of the five weeks I stayed there. Yet I couldn't have kept it together without the hospital. I wouldn't be here to tell the tale."

"I had decided that I was a lesbian, my marrriage ended, and I was in turmoil. My therapist didn't say much of anything, and I became frantic. I couldn't sleep or eat. I thought about hurting myself. I was feeling more and more out of control. Luckily, my mother insisted that I go to a local crisis clinic. I got some medication and found an active, goal-oriented therapist. I got myself together again."

◆ Task 2 ◆
Reflect on Your Working Relationship with Your Therapist

A good working relationship with your therapist is the base upon which your therapy rests. Once you have reviewed how well you and your therapist are working together, you can sort out your reactions to your therapy.

How Well Are You and Your Therapist Working Together?

As you think about your relationship now, consider the part each of you has in building your relationship and how well you are doing as a team. Are you using the basic skills that you developed during the beginning and middle phases of therapy? (See pages 79 and 116 to refresh your memory.)

I am (satisfied) (dissatisfied) with our therapeutic relationship because

When I think about my part in our relationship, I realize that I (check the column that reflects your thinking)

Often	Sometimes	Rarely	
☐	☐	☐	share the important events and concerns of my life with my therapist.
☐	☐	☐	am receptive to what is said about me in therapy.
☐	☐	☐	am able to ask my therapist questions.
☐	☐	☐	figure out what I want and need from my therapist.
☐	☐	☐	give my therapist feedback about my reactions to therapy.

I could do more to improve our relationship by

I think that my therapist (check the appropriate column)

Often	Sometimes	Rarely	
☐	☐	☐	has my best interests at heart.
☐	☐	☐	accepts me.
☐	☐	☐	understands me.
☐	☐	☐	takes me seriously.
☐	☐	☐	is knowledgeable and skillful.
☐	☐	☐	does not let his or her problems intrude on my therapy.
☐	☐	☐	is a warm, caring person.
☐	☐	☐	believes in my abilities.
☐	☐	☐	takes my feedback into account.
☐	☐	☐	does not insist on using techniques that I find objectionable.
☐	☐	☐	respects my autonomy.
☐	☐	☐	is on my side even when challenging my behavior or ideas.
☐	☐	☐	is willing to be involved in a close yet professional relationship with me.

My therapist could improve our relationship by

A good working relationship means that you and your therapist work as a team in your behalf.

As a team, we (check the column that best describes how the two of you work together)

Often	Sometimes	Rarely	
☐	☐	☐	understand each other.
☐	☐	☐	can work out disagreements.
☐	☐	☐	bring up difficult ideas.
☐	☐	☐	respect each other's point of view.
☐	☐	☐	create new ideas or solutions to my problems.
☐	☐	☐	have good rapport.
☐	☐	☐	agree on my therapy goals.

My therapist and I make a (good) (poor) (adequate) team because

We need to improve

I need to talk with my therapist about

If you do not think that you and your therapist are working well together, what does your therapist think? He or she may agree and recommend a consultation with another therapist. (See Task 5, on consultations.) On the other hand, your therapist may suggest that some unresolved issues from your past are affecting your relationship.

Your Negative Reactions to Your Therapist

As you thought about your relationship with your therapist, you may have noted negative reactions that you have toward him or her. Sorting out which of these reactions is based on the realities of your relationship and which are confounded by old patterns of thinking and feeling stirred up by the therapy experience itself can be quite a challenge.

How can you tell which feelings relate to here-and-now events with your therapist and which have to do with reactions transferred from the past? (See page 118 for a discussion of transference.) Sometimes your reactions may be a response to your therapist's lack of skill or poor handling of a situation. Your therapist may be bringing his or her own distortions and reactions into your sessions in a way that may not be helpful for you. Therapists are human and are also subject to transference reactions (in a therapist, these reactions are often called counter-transference).

Sometimes your unhappiness with other people can be displaced onto your therapist. Many therapists consider this an important opportunity to use the therapeutic relationship to promote understanding and change. Sometimes you will find that both you and your therapist play a part in your negative reaction.

Try the next exercises to sort out how your current reactions to your therapist may be affected by thoughts or feelings that originated elsewhere.

What bothers me about my therapist is

My therapist thinks that I am troubled by this because

My therapist is a lot like

My reactions to my therapist remind me of

If your reactions to your therapist echo something from your past, you'll probably want to explore this as a part of your therapy. The following statements provide further clues to the possibility that your negative reaction contains elements of unresolved reactions to past issues. Check any that resonate for you.

_____ I was comfortable with my therapist during the initial phase of therapy and became discontent as more painful issues emerged.
_____ I have a history of being dissatisfied in therapy.
_____ I usually become dissatisfied with people at some point.
_____ I am frequently unhappy with relationships.
_____ It takes a long time for me to feel comfortable with someone.
_____ The quality that upsets me in my therapist is something that I react strongly to in other people.

If any of these strike home, transference may be at work. Give it some time, to see if increased understanding changes what bothers you about your therapist.

If your dissatisfaction continues, there are some ideas for you in the next sections.

◆ Task 3 ◆
Sort Out Your Reactions to Therapy

Even if your relationship with your therapist is going well, you may wonder if your therapy could be improved. The following exercises will guide you as you sort through your reactions to your therapy and will suggest areas that you can discuss with your therapist.

What Changes Would You Like in Your Therapy?

When you filled out your Therapist Preference Chart on page 55, you decided what you wanted from your therapist. Review the chart and compare what you wanted then with what you actually have now.

As I think about my sessions, I would like (check the column that reflects your thinking)

More	Less	Same	
☐	☐	☐	focus on present-day problems.
☐	☐	☐	opportunity to decide what to talk about.
☐	☐	☐	feedback on why I do what I do.
☐	☐	☐	opportunity to talk.
☐	☐	☐	information about my problems.
☐	☐	☐	exploration of my fantasies and dreams.
☐	☐	☐	understanding of how my past influences my life.
☐	☐	☐	help in dealing with difficult behavior.
☐	☐	☐	permission to experience strong feelings during sessions.

I wish my therapy would be (check the appropriate column)

More	Less	Same	
☐	☐	☐	stimulating
☐	☐	☐	calming
☐	☐	☐	challenging
☐	☐	☐	accepting
☐	☐	☐	enlightening
☐	☐	☐	directive
☐	☐	☐	encouraging
☐	☐	☐	advice-giving
☐	☐	☐	supportive
☐	☐	☐	confrontational

I would like my therapy to shift because

What Is the Focus of Your Therapy?

Now that you have experience in therapy, what was important to you when you started may or may not continue to be important to you.

On page 17 you described your therapy goals. Have they evolved as your interests and needs have changed:

My therapy (generally addresses) (sometimes focuses on) (ignores) the issues most important to me

I leave sessions (with a sense of accomplishment) (sometimes satisfied) (doubting) that I have accomplished anything

I would like the focus of my therapy to be

If you think that your sessions are not really addressing your important concerns, see if you can figure out why.

In discussing my therapy goals with my therapist, I

What Other Possibilities Can You Consider?

You and your therapist may decide to consider other aspects of your therapy as well. For example, if you are concerned about how your sessions are scheduled, you may decide to take a look at this area more closely. Or you and your therapist may find that including or changing to individual, group, couple, or family therapy will add a new dimension to your therapy. (Turn back to page 49 and review the possible advantages of each type of therapy from your current perspective.)

◆

"We had done really well after two years of couple therapy. Toward the end of it, I kept bringing up my personal issues. The therapist and I decided that it was time for me to start individual therapy."

"Dr. K said that the increasing number and urgency of my phone calls suggested that I need to come to therapy more. Adding an extra session each week has made a big difference. I am calmer now and more on top of my life."

"I kept thinking about quitting group and going back to individual sessions only. It took a while to see that I was scared about how much I had let the group know about problems that I usually keep hidden."

"During four years of individual therapy, I complained about my husband's insensitivity, his coldness, that he seemed just like my father. My therapist suggested that my husband come with me for a while. In two sessions of couples' therapy, I got down to my part in the mess between us. I could no longer hide behind a wall of words."

"By missing so many sessions, I was sending a message that I really did not need to come twice a week anymore. Now that I've cut back, I never miss. Maybe next time I want a change, I'll know enough to say something. Since I have to pay for missed sessions, that was a very expensive way to make my point."

◆

If you would like your therapy to change, let your therapist know what you want and why you think it will help. Your requests may not be honored, but you can expect to get a respectful hearing and you should end up with an understanding of why your therapist thinks that change is or is not a good idea.

In the course of your discussion, your therapist may suggest that your concerns reflect another issue that you are struggling with or another conflict in your therapy. If you ask for advice, for example, your therapist may wonder if you are expressing a wish for more tangible evidence that he or she cares about you. If you keep wanting to change your appointment time, it may be a way for you to feel more control. Keep an open mind during these discussions and see if your therapist's ideas strike a chord.

You may end up agreeing with your therapist. If you still think that what your therapist has to offer and what you want are too far apart, you may choose to transfer to someone with a different therapeutic approach. If you are headed in this direction, you can schedule a consultation (see page 166) with another therapist to help you decide.

◆ Task 4 ◆
Consider Your Therapist's Competence and Professional Behavior

Although most therapists are competent and conduct themselves professionally with clients, some behave in unhelpful or even harmful ways. Having a bad experience in therapy is demoralizing; it can leave us doubtful of our judgment and fearful that no one can help.

If you have serious questions about whether your therapist is meeting his or her obligations to you, do not hesitate to have a consultation with another therapist to discuss your misgivings. The consultant can help you to gain some perspective on what is happening, give you the encouragement you need to get out of a hurtful situation, and suggest where you can find a new therapist who can help you to undo any damage done by your bad experience.

The descriptions below show a range of situations in which therapists have behaved in unethical, unprofessional, incompetent, or harmful ways. If any of them apply to you, your therapist may be doing more harm than good.

YOU AND YOUR THERAPIST ARE SEXUALLY INVOLVED

No therapeutic justification exists for a therapist's having a relationship that involves overtly sexual behavior with a client. A sexual relationship exploits a client and is unethical as well as illegal. (For further discussion of appropriate physical contact, see page 105.)

If you are engaged in a sexual relationship with your therapist, you may be filled with self-doubt and confusion. Talk with someone else about what is going on—a friend whom you trust, your physician, or another therapist. With support, you can find a good therapist who will help you heal from your experience.

◆

*"He said that being sexual with him would help me. He had helped
me with so many other things that I wanted to believe him. But
soon I began to feel guilty and he acted like that was part of my
problem. Finally I spoke to a friend, and she got me to see her
therapist. It was like a spell had been broken and I was free."*

◆

YOUR THERAPIST IS PREJUDICED

Therapists are subject to the same prejudices as all of us. Do you
belong to a population that has been subjected to prejudice? If your
therapist has demonstrated bias against your sex, race, age, sexual orientation, or class, and he or she is unwilling to struggle with and overcome the bias, you may need to move on.

◆

*"He often said that women do this, while men do that. He began to
annoy me with the men and women divisions on everything. When
I raised it with him, he suggested that I was having trouble with
my femininity. I just didn't want to be labeled all the time, so I
left."*

*"She came right out and said that gay men could not have mature
relationships because of their narcissism."*

◆

YOU ARE ENGAGED IN PROTRACTED CONFLICT WITH YOUR THERAPIST

If you have spent considerable time discussing your difficulties with
your therapist with no resolution, read on.

Continual conflict can occur because of either a client's or a therapist's issues or because of difficulties that both are having in the relationship. Resolving conflict can be an important part of therapy (see
page 124). Yet continued and protracted problems can become all-
consuming, taking the place of therapeutic work. In this instance, a
consultation can be particularly valuable in sorting out whether the
conflict can be resolved or you need to move on and work with a new
therapist.

◆

"I was upset with Evie for favoring my husband over me in our couples' therapy. I just couldn't let go of it and kept bringing it up at every session. She said that she tried to be evenhanded, but I still felt she just couldn't put herself in my place. Finally, my husband confessed that he'd agreed with me all along. We both figured that we'd better start over with someone new."

"My therapist was so adamant about me leaving my difficult and sometimes abusive husband that she wouldn't listen to any of my thoughts or feelings."

"My problems seemed to infuriate her. Whether I was having trouble with my wife or was too passive with my boss, my therapist would get impatient or just plain mad. She seemed to expect me to never do it again. I felt disliked and all stuck in the mire."

◆

YOUR THERAPIST IS COLD, DISTANT, AND UNREACHABLE

Any therapist, no matter what approach to therapy he or she practices, must be capable of forming a relationship. Empathy and understanding are essential ingredients in any relationship. A therapist who can't supply this—or can't for you—is not competent to help you.

◆

"Dr. P. was cold and rigid. When I told him he just did not behave like a human being, he ignored me. I felt numbed by the experience."

"He was right about a lot of what he said about me, but he said it with such disdain! At first I thought I was being hypersensitive. Then my mother died, and he implied that my pain was all unresolved anger with her. That did it. I left and am working with someone else, who is much warmer."

◆

YOUR THERAPIST IS NO LONGER COMPETENT

The most competent person can be affected by life events and have difficulty functioning. Something can change in your therapist's life so that he or she is no longer able to work with you. You may be aware that your therapist is under stress because of an illness or a difficult life event, or you may begin to notice in subtle ways that he or she can no longer function effectively.

◆

"As her illness grew worse, her attention wandered. Still she denied that anything was wrong. I really loved her, yet I could not tell her how sad I was for her, how much I wished that she could confide in me after all I had shared with her.

"As the sessions grew too full of pretense for me to bear, I told her that I was doing so well that I was taking a break from my psychotherapy. She agreed. Several months later, I heard that she had died of cancer."

"Jack, a recovered alcoholic, understood me and my fight with drinking. Then he began slipping; someone told me that they'd seen him in a neighborhood bar. When I confronted him, he said that he was able to drink socially now. When I noticed that his kitchen garbage bag was full of beer cans, I quit with the help of my AA group."

◆

YOUR THERAPIST MAKES IMMORAL, ILLEGAL, OR
HARMFUL SUGGESTIONS

Do not continue to see a therapist who encourages you to do things that are immoral, illegal, or against your best interests. If you have any questions about your therapist's ethics, a consultation is in order.

◆

"After he proposed that we file for two extra sessions a week on my insurance and split the money, my therapy was tainted."

"When I talked about being inhibited during sex, she kept asking if I turned on or used coke. After a while it was clear that using

drugs was her solution to sexual problems. I told her that I didn't need to pay seventy-five dollars an hour for advice that I could get on the street corner."

◆

YOUR THERAPIST'S PERSONAL LIFE INTRUDES

Some therapists make casual personal remarks that are benign and do not disrupt the therapy. Other therapists talk about their personal life to clarify a point or illustrate something. But your therapist and his or her life should not be the focus of your work in therapy or your attention outside it.

◆

"Ellen always talked about herself a lot during sessions, but when she began to ask my advice, and then asked me out to breakfast when she and her husband broke up, I stopped feeling flattered and started feeling exploited."

◆

If you want to know more about what is considered unethical or unprofessional, contact the professional organization to which your therapist belongs (see "Resources," page 229) or your local or county mental health association. If you determine that your therapist's behavior is unethical or unprofessional, you can report this to the board of ethics of the appropriate professional organization, the local or county mental health association, or the professional licensing department in your state.

◆ Task 5 ◆
Use a Consultation if Needed

A consultation is a discussion with a therapist *about* therapy without an agreement to engage *in* therapy. Like seeing a medical doctor for a second opinion, you can use a consultation with another therapist to discuss doubts you have about your therapy. If you have evaluated your therapy, discussed matters thoroughly with your therapist, and remain confused or troubled, a consultation is a useful next step.

A consultant can offer a fresh point of view and help you to think through your doubts and answer your questions. You may be considering consulting another therapist for any number of reasons. If you have talked with your therapist and are still unclear about how to resolve your dissatisfactions, you may use the consultation to pinpoint what is wrong and to suggest possible solutions. You may use a consultation to sort out why you and your therapist have a poor working relationship and how it might be improved. Speaking with another therapist is a must if your therapist is engaging in unprofessional or unethical behavior. A consultant can help you move out of a hurtful situation and into therapy with someone new who will help you to recover from what has happened.

Discuss the Idea with Your Therapist

Although you may feel hesitant to raise with your therapist the possibility of getting a second opinion, discussing your reasons for seeking a consultation may help clarify your concerns and inform you about your therapist's point of view.

Your therapist could welcome a second opinion. He or she may also feel that something is amiss in your therapy and be interested in the ideas a third party can offer. Your therapist may feel that it is time for a change and that a different therapist might provide something for you that he or she cannot. While it is most common for a family therapist to call in a consultant to gain a new perspective on the treatment of a family, on occasion other therapists also request and participate in consultations.

If your therapist treats your wish for a consultation as grist for the therapeutic mill, it is worth exploring his or her suggestions about what is occurring. Should your therapist react more defensively, feeling accused of failing with you, take the time to talk it out. Neither of these responses need preclude your seeking a consultation; you can continue your dialogue with your therapist while you seek another opinion.

I want to consult another therapist because

My therapist's reaction to my getting a second opinion is

Locate an Appropriate Consultant

Taking the time to choose an appropriate consultant is very important, because you will get different information depending upon the consultant you choose. If you have a question about the approach of your therapy, a consultation with a therapist of another theoretical persuasion can give you some ideas about what that other approach might offer you. However, keep in mind that a consultant may favor his or her particular school of therapy and may not be well informed about or understand your current therapist's approach.

If the type of therapy you are in seems right, but you have some question about your therapist and how you are working together, finding a consultant who shares your therapist's approach will be useful. If you are concerned about your therapist's ethics, the professional organization your therapist belongs to or your local or county mental health association may provide a consultation focused on this issue.

You can use the information in the Resource section to obtain the name of a consultant therapist. You can also ask your therapist for a recommendation. This will be especially useful if you are interested in figuring out how you and your therapist can work together more effectively, because your therapist is more likely to accept such a consultant's opinion.

Plan for Your Consultation

Just as you prepared for your first visit to a therapist by thinking about what to say and what to ask, making some advance preparation will help assure that you get what you want from this consultation.

You'll want to let the consultant know something about yourself:

- A brief description of yourself and your history.
- Your reasons for entering therapy.

- Your therapy goals.
- A brief description of your history in therapy.
- Your reasons for this consultation.

You'll also want to ask the consultant questions relevant to your particular situation:

- What are the benefits of your current therapy?
- What could be improved upon?
- Is there any way in which you are being harmed?
- What does he or she recommend?

How to Evaluate the Consultation

Take your time to review carefully what you learned from the consultation.

The consultant suggested

I have the following reactions to what the consultant said

When I shared my thoughts about the consultation with my therapist, he or she said

Neither your therapist nor the consultant is infallible. It is up to you to evaluate the usefulness of what the consultant had to say. The consultant gives you his or her best assessment, knowing you only for a brief time and your therapy only as you describe it.

◆

"Even though our family therapist discouraged me from getting individual therapy, I knew it would help. I saw another family therapist for a second opinion, and she agreed."

"Nothing much was happening in my therapy, so my therapist suggested that we go together to see his supervisor. She saw right away that my therapist was backing off whenever I started to get angry; my criticism was intimidating him. He got a lot tougher after that. My therapy stopped being so polite and got a lot more real."

"I just didn't think that the consultant tried to understand what my problems were with the group. He just kept suggesting that I needed more intensive work and implied that he was just the one to do it. I felt he was competing with my therapist."

"I felt that Josie didn't know what she was doing. She seemed to be winging it most of the time. After ten minutes with another therapist, I could see that I was right. The consultant was in charge and I felt safe. I switched therapists."

◆

Make a Decision

What do you want to happen next in your therapy? The information from your consultation and the information you have gathered throughout the evaluation process can help you and your therapist to decide how to proceed.

- You may have some possible solutions to your difficulties and be eager to put them into effect. (It may be helpful to return to Chapters 7 and 8.)
- You may be unclear and want to extend your therapy as you continue the evaluation process. (Return to this chapter as needed for guidance.)
- You may decide that your current therapy is no longer appropriate and search for a new, more suitable treatment. (Turn to Chapter 11 for help in saying goodbye, and then return to Chapters 3 and 4 to help you find a new therapist.)
- You may have confirmed that your therapy is on the right track and continue on your journey feeling reassured.

•10•

Is It Time to Leave Therapy?

TASKS

---

1. **Assess Your Progress**
2. **Discuss Ending Therapy**
3. **Make a Decision**

Just how will you know when you have gotten what you need from therapy? Most people think about leaving from time to time during the course of their therapy. You may worry that you will leave too soon or stay when you are getting little from the experience. It is not always easy to decide when to end therapy, but a careful assessment can make a difference. Bringing your concerns into your therapy will make the process of deciding an opportunity for self-exploration and growth. This chapter will help you determine whether you are ready to leave therapy. The next chapter will guide you through the ending itself.

Getting your thoughts and feelings down in black and white is a good place to start. Be sure and take your time with the exercises in this chapter. Whether it requires hours or even days, write down everything that occurs to you. It will be valuable information for you and your therapist to use in making your decision.

I am considering ending therapy now because (check any statements that reflect your situation)

____ I have gotten a lot from my therapy and feel satisfied.

____ I keep thinking about leaving.

____ My friends or family want me to stop.

_____ I (or my therapist) cannot continue because of outside circumstances.

_____ Nothing much has happened in my therapy for quite a while.

_____ My therapist and I are not working well together.

_____ I think that I've gotten all I can from working with this therapist.

_____ I've gotten most of what I want, and it doesn't seem worthwhile
to continue.

_____ My therapist suggested that I should think about leaving.

_____ I don't have the time or money to continue.

_____ or, _____

My reservations about leaving therapy are

◆

*"I've been in group therapy for many years. I've often thought
about quitting and actually said so a couple of times. As I look
back I can see that for me each discussion about quitting was a
kind of plateau in which I reassessed my progress and obtained a
new understanding of where I'd been and where I wanted to go."*

*"We started family sessions because our older son was giving us a
lot of trouble. We all get along better now. My husband and I are
more in charge with the kids, and we take more time for
ourselves."*

*"As I think about leaving therapy, I notice that I feel lighter. It's
not that I've lost weight; it's just that I'm not carrying around so
much psychological baggage."*

◆ Task 1 ◆
Assess Your Progress

We would all like to leave therapy having gotten the most possible
from the experience. While you may have assessed your progress at
other points, now is the time for a thorough review. If you are having a

hard time seeing how your growth has evolved over time, remembering what you were like before you began therapy can help you pinpoint the changes you have made. Review Chapters 1 and 2 to refresh your memory. Then look at the goals that you set for yourself at the beginning of therapy on page 17. If you did an evaluation of your therapy, turn to page 151 and note what you wrote about your progress then.

Now write about the gains you have made and add any issues that still need work. You might pretend that you are the benevolent friend that you have employed at other times to help you be objective about yourself.

Since beginning therapy, I feel better about

I would still like to deal with

◆

"When I started analysis I was an anxious wreck. Getting some relief was all I cared about. As I calmed down, I realized I was upset about my marriage and my problems at work. A year and a half into my analysis, Dr. H. helped me see how conflicted I was about being a success and surpassing my father. I couldn't believe how often that theme kept appearing. I am clearer and feel much better now."

"I understand now why it's so hard to do research on the outcome of treatment. What has changed mostly for me is my attitude. I just experience things differently. I feel better. It means everything to me."

"After my mother died suddenly, I saw a therapist because of my insomnia. Now I feel more accepting of my mother's death, but I still sleep poorly."

"I'm bitterly disappointed by how little I've gotten so far. Why should I keep putting in good time and money if nothing is going to change?"

"When I began therapy, my dreams were filled with images of me treading water. After being in therapy awhile, my dreams changed; I would be holding on to a fat inner tube that I wore around my waist. Now, as I am ready to leave, my dreams have me on solid ground."

◆

Use the next exercise to see if you are contented with the changes that you have made and are satisfied with the important areas of your life. Keep in mind that there is no such thing as perfection. These statements represent how you'll feel most of the time when you are ready to leave therapy.

Most of the time
_____ I am happy about the progress that I've made in dealing with the issues that brought me to therapy.
_____ I accept myself.
_____ I like the way that I get along with my lover, spouse, friends, family, and co-workers.
_____ I accept responsibility for myself and do not blame others for who I am.
_____ I am able to think clearly.
_____ I am aware of and accept my feelings.
_____ I am satisfied with my sex life.
_____ I have caring relationships.
_____ I avoid self-defeating behavior.
_____ My goals are realistic and reachable.
_____ My work is fulfilling.
_____ I like the way I take care of myself.
_____ I am cooperative with others.
_____ I can deal with the problems in my life and know how to find help if I need it.
_____ I am hopeful about my future.

Becoming Your Own Therapist

You may find yourself using the tools for success in therapy and practicing the skills and gathering the information you need to continue

on your own. The process of learning to be your own therapist probably
has been uneven and slow, but as you look back, you may be surprised
by how far you have come.

How are you doing at becoming your own therapist?

I am often able to

_____ rely on myself more and my therapist less.

_____ figure out the part I play in my problems.

_____ know how to deal with my feelings constructively.

_____ reassure, support, and encourage myself.

_____ be empathic with myself and others.

_____ think through my problems.

_____ understand why I behave, feel, and think the way I do.

_____ set appropriate limits on my behavior.

_____ see which of my current reactions are transferred from the past
and which are appropriate to the current situation.

_____ or, _____

Look through the areas that you did not check and think about
what more you might want to do.

Now that you have had the chance to develop an overview of where
you are now, it is time to bring your thoughts and feelings to your
therapist.

◆ Task 2 ◆
Discuss Ending Therapy

Discussing ending a therapy relationship may be uncomfortable for
client and therapist alike, and both may be tempted to avoid the subject. You may think that discussing "termination" (therapists' jargon for
ending therapy) should happen only when you are 100 percent ready
to leave, or you may be concerned about hurting your therapist's feelings or incurring his or her anger.

Talk to your therapist about termination whenever the idea occurs
to you. This continuing communication enriches therapy, while it helps
both of you to be clear about the right time for you to end.

I imagine my therapist's response to my leaving therapy will be

The subject of ending therapy may take place over many sessions. Your therapist will want to understand thoroughly why you feel ready to leave now. While some therapists let clients know immediately what they think about their readiness to leave, others believe that it is important to explore a client's feelings and reasoning fully before sharing their own thoughts.

After you have started the discussion of your possible departure from therapy, compare how you thought your therapist would react with his or her actual response.

My therapist's reactions to my leaving are

We need to continue talking about

If both of you agree that you are approaching the end of your sessions together, you are ready to begin the ending phase of your therapy. Turn to the next chapter, where you can learn about the process of terminating.

You may be surprised to find out that your therapist does not agree and wants you to stay! Or you may discover that your therapist is encouraging you to consider ending therapy before you feel ready. The rest of this chapter can give you some ideas about how you can work together to learn from your differences.

Is It Too Soon for You to Leave?

It may be unsettling and disappointing to learn that your therapist doesn't share your assessment of your progress or agree that you are ready to leave therapy. There can be a number of reasons that your therapist has taken that position.

• *Your therapist wants more for you.* Perhaps you feel that you have gotten as much as you can from therapy. You may have met your goals and feel satisfied with your progress. Yet your therapist may believe that you can achieve even more. Ask your therapist to review your progress with you and to suggest clearly what more you might get from continuing therapy.

My therapist would like me to continue therapy so that I can

• *Another issue is influencing your decision.* Your therapist may suggest that something is going on in your life or in therapy that is leading you to want to leave therapy before you are actually finished. Below are some reasons that lead people to quit therapy prematurely. Check any of the statements that resonate for you.

_____ *I am under a lot of stress.* (When things are rough, you may clean house by getting rid of people, and your therapist may be no exception.)

Do any of these statements sound familiar? "I broke up with my lover / spouse." "I quit my job." "I argued with my best friend."

_____ *Everyone is leaving me.* (You may want to regain some control by showing your therapist how it feels to be left.)

Do you recognize yourself in any of these quotes? "School is over." "My boyfriend and I broke up." "My best friend moved." "I've been fired."

_____ *I don't really deserve all that I have now.* (You may be uncomfortable about the gains that you've made and be sabotaging your forward motion. See page 126 on overcoming obstacles to change.)

Do these statements reflect your feelings? "I feel guilty about having more than others." "I am frightened; people will be envious."

_____ *I'm losing my independence.* (You may need some distance because you are getting too close to your therapist or group. See page 116 for a discussion of issues of intimacy and separateness.)

Have you been thinking the following? "If I trust, they may leave me. It's better if I leave first." "If I stay, I'll lose my individuality."

_____ *I am angry with my therapist.* (You may be protecting others from your anger.)

Do these statements reflect your circumstances? "I feel hurt by something my therapist has done." "My therapist has just returned from / is about to go on vacation."

_____ *I'm bored.* (Your boredom may cover up other feelings, like fear or anger. Turn back to page 120 for a discussion of what to do when you're stuck in therapy.)

Do these quotes sound like you? "Nothing is happening in my therapy." "I'm tired of listening to other people talk about their problems in group."

_____ I can't afford the (time) (travel) (fee). Real conflicts do arise involving these issues. Sometimes these issues mask other doubts or fears about therapy. Here is a way to distinguish between a reality conflict and a possible cover for something that is difficult to confront right now.

If (time) (travel) (money) or _____ were not a problem for me, I would still want to leave therapy now because

♦ *Old issues are affecting your decision.* Your therapist may believe that your wish to leave therapy has to do with unresolved issues from the past rather than the here-and-now reality. (See page 118 for an explanation of transference.)

Does your therapist view your desire to leave as a reenactment of something from your past? Get as much information as you can from him or her and then evaluate it.

My therapist suggests that my desire to leave therapy now is related to

This interpretation makes / doesn't make sense to me because

In order to clarify my understanding, I need to ask my therapist

◆

"As I look back on it now, I left because I was convinced that my therapist wanted me to marry my fiancé and I knew I needed to break off the engagement. I never checked this out with my therapist. In retrospect, it seems that he was actually open to my doing whatever I wanted about the marriage. It was my father who really wanted me married."

"The first few days of my therapist's vacation, I felt so alone and depressed. Then I got this great idea to change my life radically by moving to a new city. When my therapist returned, he helped me see that my wanting to leave had to do with getting back at him for leaving me and upsetting me so. He said that I'm particularly sensitive to separations because my mother left me a lot when I was little. I get like that. I want to leave when I've been left."

◆

• ***A sudden decision makes your motives suspect.*** If you are struck with the impulse to leave therapy, you may be trying to avoid a painful subject, memory, or feeling. It can feel temporarily relieving to decide to leave rather than deal with this pain.

If you are having a hard time in therapy and then find yourself deciding to terminate, it is worth rethinking your decision to leave. Sometimes this avoidance takes the form of feeling fine and believing that all old difficulties have disappeared. Some therapists call this a "flight into health."

If I am avoiding something difficult or painful now, it might be

◆

"We had worked on my feelings about myself and my career and my therapist started asking about my relationship with my husband. At first I thought: I've made enough progress and I want to leave. Then my therapist said she thought I wanted to leave because I was too scared to talk about my marriage. I decided to trust her and stay in therapy. Our marriage would not have lasted had she not said anything and let me leave. Now I am really ready to end therapy."

◆

Are You Hanging on Too Long?

Your therapist may think that you are ready to try your wings, while you think that you have more to gain from therapy. Take the time to find out why your therapist thinks that you are ready to leave now; even if you disagree, you may learn something from your therapist's perspective. There are a number of reasons people hang on to their therapy. Has your therapist suggested that any of them apply to you?

• **Therapy as substitute for living.**   Is your therapy so satisfying or so comforting that you have little need for anything else in your life? Your relationship with your therapist or group should serve as a bridge to closer connections with others rather than as a substitute for these relationships.

• **Perfection-seeking.**   Are you waiting until you are perfect? You may have hoped that with therapy you would make no more mistakes, feel no more pain or fear. Leaving therapy may mean that you have to accept your limitations. You may be sad, angry, or relieved as you give up your fantasies of perfection.

• **Taking all the blame.**   Are you most comfortable believing that you are the problem rather than facing a hard reality? You may have experienced an abusive spouse, dead-end employment, a family lacking in emotional resources, or problems resulting from sexism, racism, or the economy. The idea of confronting some kind of change outside yourself can be terrifying. Taking the rap can help you avoid a more difficult separation, like leaving your parents, spouse, or job.

Do you usually blame yourself? This is the time in therapy to accept that no amount of work on yourself will change certain impossible situations. It may be time to let go of and mourn the disappointing reality. (See page 120 for a discussion of this subject.)

• *Flight from separation.*   Do you hate to say goodbye? Have you noticed a problem with separating in other situations?

If you are aware that you have gotten what you came for and that very little new is happening in your therapy, you may be avoiding separation. If separation is an issue for you, a carefully planned termination can provide the time and space for you to resolve separation issues.

• *Fear of disapproval.*   A corollary of the flight from separation is staying in therapy to avoid real or imagined disapproval. You may feel grateful to your therapist or loyal to the members of your group and believe that it would be hurtful to leave them.

I might stay in therapy longer than I need because

After some discussion, you may decide that your therapist's assessment makes sense and that this is a good time to leave. On the other hand, your therapist may decide that you have more to gain and will continue your therapy or refer you to another therapist. For a number of clients, therapy provides a needed resource unavailable in their families or their communities, and, by necessity, the course of their treatment may cover a great many years. Many therapists recognize this and are willing to continue working with clients who need long-term therapy. If your therapist practices in a way that precludes this possibility and you think that you need to continue your therapy, speak with your current therapist about transferring to a therapist who can see you for a longer period of time.

◆

"I had a very difficult childhood. I do have a good job, friends, a stable life, yet I am always frightened and suspicious. I need to keep checking out my thinking with someone outside the situation

in order to figure out what's going on. Some people don't understand my being in therapy for so many years, but I know that I really need it."

◆

When Other Issues Cloud Your Therapist's Judgment

Occasionally therapists who have been caring and consistent become transformed into insistent, even angry people when the subject of termination is raised. Separation provokes complex feelings for everyone, including therapists. Your therapist may have professional or personal reasons for encouraging you to stay or leave.

Other issues may cloud a therapist's judgment. The financial or personal loss when a client leaves may play a part. A therapist may be reluctant to give up a gratifying relationship with a client.

Although you could gain more from therapy, your therapist may for his or her own reasons suggest that you end your therapy. He or she may feel inadequate to address your issues or may be unable to overcome countertransference reactions (see page 157). He may be cutting back on his practice or be preoccupied with problems. Or your therapist may just be mistaken in his or her assessment of your readiness to end now.

If, after discussion, you and your therapist don't agree, you can seek a second opinion to help you decide how to proceed. (For information about obtaining a consultation, turn to page 166.)

NOTE: It can be difficult for a therapist to let you go if you are still in pain. It can be especially hard to let you end therapy if you are still self-destructive, if you are damaging someone else, or if you experience one or more of the serious symptoms on page 22. In these instances, it is not time for you to leave therapy.

I imagine my therapist's issues about my leaving are

When we discussed my fantasy, I learned

These are the questions that I still have for my therapist

◆

"I kept telling him that I wanted more. Sure I'm a better parent and my career is going well, but I still feel bad about myself. After his trying to show me that I was finished with therapy and my trying to tell him I needed more, he decided to refer me to another therapist, who could help me."

"When I decided to leave my therapeutic community, my therapist told me that there was no hope for me to change unless I stayed with them. I left. At first it was hard for me to hold on to my own strengths. It was the right decision. If I stayed like my boyfriend did, I would be dependent on them forever."

"My therapist was scared of my husband's temper. He made nice to him and told us we were doing well enough to stop therapy. I felt cheated."

◆

Consider Other Opinions

Your therapist may not be the only one with an opinion about your readiness to leave therapy. Other important people may have strong views about your ending therapy. Is anyone encouraging you to leave therapy before you are ready or to stay in therapy longer than seems necessary?

Sometimes family, lovers, or friends are uncomfortable with our being in therapy. Many times parents or partners are frightened that they will be blamed by therapists or be criticized by us and lose our love. They may worry that something is seriously wrong and want reassurance that all is well. Once the therapy ends, they will be relieved of their fear or worry.

Other times, people may have goals for us that we don't share. Did you begin therapy because someone else was concerned about you or bothered by some aspect of your behavior? Is there someone in your life now who wants you to be different from the way you are?

Evaluating other people's feedback is a good idea. Often there may be something you can learn. If someone in your life has an opinion about whether you ought to stay in or leave therapy, use the next exercises to consider his or her thinking. In the process, ask yourself if you have been talking with them about your therapy in a way that would encourage them to over- or undervalue it.

_____ (insert name) recommends that I (stay in) (leave) (change to) another therapy because

My therapist thinks I (ought to consider) (can proceed in spite of) this recommendation because

◆

"I am so self-destructive at times that the only reason I stay in therapy, or stay alive, for that matter, is because I know my therapist and my group really care about me. Even though I am staying for them, I suppose I'm really staying for myself."

"I've been in therapy for a year now, and I still don't think my being turned on to kids, fondling them and having them touch me is so bad. It's not like I'm having intercourse with them. The only reason that I go to therapy is that my wife will leave me if I don't."

"My husband wants me to stay in therapy so I will be more 'cooperative' with him. That sounds reasonable, except what he means by cooperative is really submissive. He can't stand how I've learned to be myself since therapy has begun."

◆ Task 3 ◆
Make a Decision

Having thought through why you want to leave and what more you might get from continuing, you may feel better equipped to make your decision. You can take your therapist's opinion and the desires of other people into account, but under most circumstances, it is up to you to make the decision for yourself.

Keep in mind that deciding to leave does not mean that you end immediately. Following your decision, you will begin the termination phase of your therapy, during which you will have the chance to say a thoughtful goodbye. The next chapter will guide you in this process.

When External Circumstances Dictate Your Ending

In some cases, the decision to end therapy is not yours to make. You may be going to a clinic where the total number of sessions is limited or where therapists leave their jobs or complete their training and move on. Something in your or your therapist's life may interfere with the continuation of your therapy.

◆

"My therapist told me that he was leaving the clinic, and that if I wanted to I could be 'transferred' to another therapist. I felt like an object being passed on to someone else."

"I got this great job in another city and had to leave therapy. But I just wasn't ready. My therapist worked out a way for me to see him once a month and have phone sessions until ending seems right."

"I will miss my group; after four years they are like a family to me. I love and trust my therapist; if only she weren't moving and disbanding the group. I've been crying for months. She says that I can go to marathon group sessions after she's moved, but it will never be the same."

◆

Your therapist may ask you to leave because you are breaking important rules. Usually your therapist will have suggestions about where you can go to get further assistance.

◆

"I was an undergraduate and I was broke all the time. The counseling center only charged five dollars a session, but I never had it. The counselor said that I didn't seem to care enough about therapy to make it a priority and to come back when I was ready to work."

"We could not be high and come to group. When I continued to drink right before sessions, the therapist told me I couldn't come back again and gave me the name of a good alcoholism program."

◆

What Have You Decided?

Review what you have learned, and then answer the following questions.

It is better for me to continue my therapy now because

I am going to take a break from my therapy because

I am ready to begin the process of leaving therapy now because

I am going to continue discussing ending my therapy because

Take the Time for an Ending Phase of Therapy

Whatever you have decided, you have just gone through a very important process of self-exploration. If you are staying in therapy, turn back to Chapters 7 and 8 and continue your journey. If you have decided to leave, you will be embarking on the final phase of your therapy. Even if the decision to end your therapy has been marked by conflict with your therapist or is beyond your control, it is worthwhile to go through as much of a termination process as circumstances permit. You have a lot to gain by a carefully considered leave-taking. Be sure to read the next chapter before you actually end your therapy.

·11·
Leaving Therapy

Now that you have decided to end therapy, an important part of your work lies ahead—the actual leave-taking. This final phase of your therapy is just as important as the beginning and middle phases; a thoughtful, fully experienced ending will protect and extend all the work you've done so far.

A great deal may happen between your decision to end and the last session. Like preparing to leave home, you need time to get used to the idea of leaving a safe and familiar place that holds personal history and meaning. You will have a chance to pack what you want to take along, plan for your new life, tie up all the loose ends, reminisce, and say goodbye. This chapter guides you through all of this.

◆ Task 1 ◆
Explore Your Reactions to Ending Therapy

Endings stir up complicated feelings in all of us. During the last phase of therapy, you are dealing with ending an important relationship and at the same time you may be struggling with the ghosts of past endings.

This ending can be painful, bittersweet, joyous, a great relief, or a combination of these feelings. To avoid dealing with these feelings you may be tempted to continue as usual. Sessions may go by without mentioning the upcoming ending. You or your therapist may be tempted to ignore, run away from, or rush through this final phase of therapy. Make your reactions a part of your therapy so that the process will be a rich one for you. Use this time for your benefit. Neither rush the ending nor prolong it.

The next exercise helps you be aware of what you feel as you end this experience. Check as many statements as apply and use the blank space to write about them if you like.

As I contemplate ending therapy I feel

_____ satisfied with my experience in therapy.
_____ relieved that I no longer have to go to sessions.
_____ disappointed that I haven't gotten more from therapy.
_____ proud of how far I've come.
_____ angry because I have to leave.
_____ sad to leave my therapist or group.
_____ excited about the future.
_____ impatient to see what it will be like without therapy.
_____ pleased that I will have more time and money for myself.
_____ scared that I will be abandoned or rejected by my therapist.
_____ overwhelmed, lost, or frightened at the thought of being without therapy.
_____ guilty about leaving.
_____ grateful for all I've gotten.
_____ very little of anything.
_____ or, _____

Your reactions will probably change as time goes on. You may want to return to this checklist from time to time to note and understand any changes in your feelings.

◆

"When I think about ending therapy I think about a kind of death. I think of how precious the relationship is and how I will miss it.

Then, I think of a kind of rebirth; living more freely emotionally, without the commitment or expense of therapy."

"We worry that without couples' therapy we'll be jinxed back into being unpleasant and bored with each other."

"When I first decided to end, I felt nostalgic and grateful to my therapist. Then even though it was my idea to stop therapy, I found myself feeling rejected and angry. Now I feel more balanced. I like Dr. R and respect the work we've done together."

◆

The way we leave therapy is often reminiscent of how we have reacted to other important partings. Just as you did in the beginning and middle phases, explore how you usually deal with endings. Anticipating what may happen will give you more control over what actually happens.

Here are some common styles of separating. Although at first glance they may appear to be different, they have some things in common. When we adopt any one of these patterns we are attempting to make the process of leave-taking easier by minimizing the discomfort of separating. Yet, by failing to acknowledge and deal with all of our reactions, we limit the richness of the experience. As you thought back to past endings you may have identified some patterns of your own. Have you ended relationships or experiences in one or another or a mixture of these styles?

Styles of Separating

• *Avoiding goodbyes.* Often we ignore the upcoming leave-taking in the hope that we will spare ourselves (and possibly others) uncomfortable or painful feelings. We may worry that others will not care whether or not we say goodbye. Or we may be expressing our disappointment in the experience by leaving without saying farewell. Not saying goodbye is also a way of denying that it is really over.

◆

"I didn't hug my favorite camp counselor goodbye or exchange addresses with the kids in my bunk. I didn't go to my high school

graduation or let my parents drive me to college. When my favorite aunt was dying, I didn't visit her in the hospital, and I didn't go to her funeral when she died. When I decided to end therapy, I was tempted to stop coming without much discussion."

◆

• ***Using anger to separate.***   You may find yourself more at home with anger than with the other emotions that leave-taking inspires. You may feel that the anger will protect you from other more painful emotions such as longing and sadness, or even joy. Sometimes we use anger to help us justify the fact that we are ending.

◆

"I had a fight with my best friend in third grade when she moved to the suburbs. I battled my parents when I was 18 and left home. I have been fired from jobs that I didn't like by getting the boss riled. I notice that I keep trying to pick a fight with my therapist and group now that I'm discussing leaving therapy."

◆

• ***Staying around for crumbs.***   Afraid that we may miss something important by leaving, or worried that we won't be able to manage alone, we stay in a relationship longer than necessary. Yet often we stay for minimal returns.

◆

"I stick around feeling cheated and angry; I can't leave until I get what I want. I have held onto the most impossible friends, hoping they would come through. Now I am refusing to set the date to leave, always wanting something more."

◆

• ***Devaluing the past.***   It can seem easier to leave something that wasn't any good in the first place than to leave something of value. When we devalue an experience or a relationship we can cushion painful feelings about leaving since we convince ourselves that there is nothing really to miss.

◆

"I am always glad to move on. I can't imagine why I hung around so long. I don't like to waste my time thinking about the past. I feel that I got nothing out of therapy, it was a great disappointment."

◆

◆ **Denying the importance of leaving.**   We can protect ourselves from the complex feelings about leaving by minimizing the importance of leaving and not feeling much.

◆

"We moved around quite a bit when I was a kid and I don't think that separations are a problem for me. Ending therapy doesn't need to be a big deal."

◆

As I reflect on the way I've ended things in the past, I see that I

If I follow my usual pattern during the ending phase of therapy I may

I would like to end differently this time by

Doubts About Leaving Are Common

It is possible to be eager and move on and, at the same time, to want to hold onto what is familiar and safe. Having mixed feelings about leaving therapy is to be expected in this ending phase. Do you experience any of the following signs of ambivalence? Check those statements that apply.

_____ I wonder if I can make it on my own.
_____ I thought I had worked out a problem and now it is recurring.

_____ I am finding new issues to talk about as I am leaving.

_____ I am developing new symptoms since I have decided to end.

_____ I find that there is a part of me that wants to stay in this secure relationship.

If you have checked any of these statements, be assured. These are common occurrences in the final phase of therapy. Whenever we leave something of value we will have some second thoughts.

◆

"I keep dreaming that I am climbing a rickety ladder and the rungs won't hold me. I am in constant danger of falling. That's just what I fear will happen without therapy."

"I've always held a little part of me in reserve. In the beginning of therapy I thought that when I could let myself feel that my therapist was my best friend, I'd be ready to end therapy. Now I feel that way and I don't want to leave!"

"My lover and I started having the same old fights again just before our last sessions. When we recognized what was happening, we burst out laughing because we were so sure that we had no doubts about leaving."

◆ Task 2 ◆
Plan Your Leave-Taking

How long will you and your therapist take to conclude your therapy and say goodbye? The length of the final phase of your therapy will depend on your unique situation and your therapist's approach to therapy.

If you are in a short form of therapy, you may have been discussing termination from the beginning. If you are in a setting where the ending date is predetermined, you and your therapist will be involved in planning how to use your final sessions meaningfully rather than in deciding when to end.

If your therapy has been going on for more than a year, you may spend several months talking about leaving. If your therapy is longer term, a proportionately longer time will be spent on ending. You and your therapist need to discuss what is best for you.

How would you like to end therapy? Below are some different ending plans. Discuss your choice in therapy; your therapist may recommend that one or a combination of these is best for you.

- *A gradual ending.* You taper off, seeing your therapist less frequently than usual. You may cut down to once a week, once every two weeks, or monthly. You will have a taste of what ending therapy will be like.
- *An issue oriented ending.* You and your therapist decide that you will end therapy once you finish working on a particular theme or problem. Once the work is done you will leave therapy.
- *A specific date is set.* You and/or your therapist set the ending time. Barring emergencies, you will use the allotted time to complete any unfinished business.

◆ Task 3 ◆
Complete Your Therapy

As you move through the ending phase, a lot of unexpected emotional issues may arise. Your therapy may very well accelerate or intensify in this last phase and you may be surprised by the amount you accomplish.

Tie Up Loose Ends

Is there something you want to work on before you set the date for your last session? Have you left some issue for last?

Before leaving therapy, I want to

◆

"I have saved one problem for last. I smoke a joint every night before I go to bed. After I work that one out I'll be ready to stop therapy."

"Before we leave I want us to have a couple of fights and to resolve them without resorting to deafening silence for weeks on end."

"When my daughter gets another F and I don't get depressed and blame myself, I'll know that I'm cured. I can't believe that for once I'm actually looking forward to the possibility that she will mess up just to see how I'll handle it."

◆

Review Your Therapy with Your Therapist

One of the most meaningful parts of leave-taking can be reviewing your therapy with your therapist. It gives each of you a chance to share your perspective on the work you have done.

You may find that your therapist is more forthcoming than usual. Even therapists whose style is fairly neutral may become more personal as the end of therapy approaches.

As you respond to the next statements think about what you would like to share with your therapist.

What I appreciate about my therapy with you is

I've always wanted you to know

Remember when

I wish that I

I wish that you

I would like to ask you

If others are involved in therapy with you, go through these exercises again this time keeping your partner, group, or family members in mind.

Allow Yourself to Mourn

Many of us experience a sense of loss as we face the end of therapy. You may feel mournful about leaving behind the important relationship with your therapist and the unique experience of therapy. It can be surprising to discover that you are also mourning other less expected losses. You may miss the parts of yourself that you have changed as a result of therapy as well as the unrealistic expectations for a more perfect you.

YOUR THERAPY

You may feel relieved that you no longer need therapy, yet you may also anticipate its absence as a loss.

I will miss

_____ a special time to think and talk about myself.

_____ having a place to problem solve.

_____ working with someone on my behalf.

_____ the opportunity to gain insight and awareness.

_____ the encouragement to express my feelings.

_____ knowing that someone understands.

_____ having a place to explore fantasies, dreams, and my unconscious
life.

_____ getting ideas about how to handle things.

_____ the closeness between me and my therapist or group.

_____ the acceptance and support.

_____ or, _____

YOUR THERAPIST

Take some time to think about what has been special to you about
your therapist.

What I will miss most about _____ **is**

◆

*"Don's wry humor always disarms me. Once when I was carrying
on and predicting the worst for my son, he suggested that I put
him on a preventative dose of Thorazine to fend off what was
clearly an impending psychosis. That snapped me back to reality
faster than any reassurance would have. I loved the glint in his eye
when he said that. No one else has been able to make me laugh
when I'm so full of anxiety."*

*"All of the good things that happened in therapy don't count for
anything now because I am so mad at Dr. M. I hate him for
moving and leaving me behind. He says that I'll remember the rest
later, but I'm not so sure."*

*"Even when Dr. H challenged me and confronted my stuff, I
always knew he liked and respected me. He'd hang in there with
me. Who will do that for me once therapy is over?"*

*"I will miss Emily's nurturing qualities. I never want to forget how
it felt when she gave me a hug. I felt so safe and protected."*

◆

YOUR FORMER SELF

Change can involve a sense of loss as we give up old ways of coping, feeling, thinking, and behaving. Even though the new ways may be more positive and life enhancing, we may feel sad (see page 126, "Obstacles to Change"). Do you feel that you have lost an important part of you as a result of therapy?

When I think about how I used to be, I miss

◆

"There was something beautiful about the naive, trusting way that I approached life. Sure, I got stepped on, but I had a kind of innocence that is gone."

"It's hard to explain, but having decided to live and to give up the option of suicide is a loss to me. It was like a friend that could always be there as a last resort."

◆

YOUR UNREALISTIC EXPECTATIONS

As you have thought about your gains, you may have been struck also by what you have not accomplished. Ending therapy brings us face to face with our limitations. We may have wanted to be liked by everyone, free of tumultuous feelings, unseemly behavior, or difficult daily problems. Therapy just cannot make us the ideal people we may have secretly hoped to become. Ending therapy challenges us to accept our imperfections and like who we are.

I have given up my expectation that

◆

"My mother will never love me the way that I want her to and no amount of work in therapy will change that reality."

"When I began therapy, I was sure that ultimately it would help me be a serene person, calm with my husband and kids, wise beyond my years. I think I am smarter now in a certain way, but serene? No way, there are no flies on me. I'm more outspoken and passionate than I was before. Goodbye to that serene image. It's just not who I am."

◆

Anticipate Future Hard Times

Everything cannot be tied up neatly. You can be sure that life will present you with the unexpected. Yet you may be able to foresee some issues that may be hard for you to deal with after therapy.

An old problem may recur or an event may stir up some difficulty. You may be graduating from college, having your youngest leave the nest or dealing with the death of a parent in the foreseeable future. You may worry that a particular emotional issue may recur. Imagine your future vulnerable moments and explore them in therapy now to prepare for them.

What may be hard for me in the future is

What I can do to help myself through

I might return to therapy if

◆

"My therapist and I figured out that because I survived the terrorism in my country and left everyone I love behind to suffer, I feel guilty and depressed whenever something good happens to me. I will be getting my Ph.D. after I leave therapy and want to catch myself before I drift into another depression."

"I've worked as much as I can on the problem I have with men. I can't wait around in therapy until I meet someone. If I have trouble once I get into a serious relationship, I'll just come back."

◆

Set Goals

With your therapist's help, consider your goals for the future:

1. _____

2. _____

3. _____

4. _____

I can reach my goals by

◆ Task 4 ◆
Say Goodbye

Finally, after all is said and done, the time has come for you to say goodbye. Before you see your therapist for the ending session, let yourself fantasize about how you would like your last meeting to be and describe it in the space below.

Imagine what you would like to happen in this session. Picture what you would like from your therapist, from your fellow group members or partner in couple therapy. Describe what you would like to do or say.

Now the time has come actually to say goodbye. You may find that your last session is less eventful or more moving than you expected. Complete the sentences below to describe what actually happened.

In my last session I

In my last session my group or partner

In my last session my therapist

What I will always want to remember about my last session is

How I feel about having left therapy

◆

"Everyone in group recalled a piece of work that I had done and told me what they would miss about me. Then we had champagne."

"Our last session was melancholy. There were some silences. After talking about my hopes and sadness about leaving, we shook hands warmly."

"I gave my therapist a new plant for her office and told her how grateful I was for all her care and attention."

◆

·12·
After Therapy

What can you do to continue building on the gains you made during therapy? The learning and growing that begin in therapy constitute a lifelong process. Successful therapy provides us with the knowledge and tools to deal in new and better ways with life's challenges. We can continue to employ what we have learned long after we have said goodbye to our therapists. We can also develop new resources to help us resolve problems creatively and promote our well-being. This chapter offers guidance to make the most of your life after therapy.

◆ Task 1 ◆
Be Your Own Therapist

As you contend with life on your own, you'll find many opportunities to apply the lessons you learned in therapy. It is your job now to provide for yourself what therapy once provided for you. And you may find—perhaps unexpectedly—that you are good at it.

The following statements represent aspects of what your therapist might do for you. Check those that describe how you are doing at being your own therapist, and write a sentence or two if you wish at the end of each statement.

_____ I make time to think about myself.

_____ I take my thoughts and feelings seriously.

_____ I can comfort myself.

_____ I avoid making harsh judgments about myself and others.

_____ I try to understand other people's point of view.

_____ I am pursuing my goals.

_____ I make an effort to see the part I play in any problems that I have.

_____ When a problem occurs, I manage it.

_____ I work at understanding what I think or feel.

_____ I am optimistic about solving future problems.

_____ or, _____

As we take stock of ourselves after therapy, we may be doing just fine; we handle our affairs, manage good and bad days, and deal with life's ups and downs. The experience of therapy has helped equip us to deal with whatever comes our way.

Even the most successful therapy cannot change hard realities; we all experience some rough times in our lives. You may have trouble coping with an old psychological issue you hoped had been resolved in therapy. Perhaps an unexpected challenge or difficulty has emerged, and you are unsure how to make things better. Your experience in therapy can provide a model for how you can help yourself now.

Have a Therapy Session with Yourself

If you get stuck, take some time and engage in a therapy session with yourself. Use this special time to think about how your therapist might have helped. Give yourself what your therapist would have offered you during a session. Recapturing your therapist's actual approach can help you understand and handle what's troubling you now.

During your session with yourself, put the tools for success in therapy into action (see page 137). Be curious about your problem, carefully observe yourself and the issue that concerns you, empathize with yourself and anyone else involved, and use good communication when the problem concerns another person. Think about the questions your therapist might ask you, and imagine the comments he or she might make.

If you have a problem right now, use the space below or your journal to write an imaginary dialogue between you and your former therapist. Describe the problem that bothers you, respond with your therapist's questions and your answers, and continue the imaginary dialogue in your journal until you reach some understanding or a possible solution.

How I might describe the problem to my therapist

How my therapist might respond

◆

"Whenever I'm stuck and can't resolve a messy situation, I go through the same process that I did in therapy. I tell myself that I have a good reason for staying stuck; I just don't know what it is yet. Then I begin writing down anything I can think of that would be a reason not to change, no matter how silly it seems."

"We made a plan in couples' therapy that if we start to get into a heated argument, we will take time out and write to each other in a special notebook. This plan has worked pretty well. We each get a chance to express ourselves, and I know that when I read what my husband has to say, I can attend to his ideas without being distracted by the anger on his face or in his voice. This technique we learned in therapy has kept us communicating through some hard times."

◆

If an issue, crisis, or problem comes up that is too difficult to handle on your own, you may want to touch base with therapy. Unlike the first time around, now you have a good idea of what therapy is like. In order to obtain some extra help, you may decide to consult with your former therapist or to contact a new one.

If you think returning to therapy means that therapy has failed and fear that your former therapist will be disappointed in you, you may hesitate. Keep in mind that many therapists enjoy keeping in touch with their clients, and all realize that hard times may bring a client back for a visit. A visit or two with your former therapist may help you sort through these issues. If you are considering seeing someone new, turn to page 59 for more information.

◆

"Two years after my analysis ended, I had an intense and prolonged anxiety attack in anticipation of the removal of a benign mole from my face. It took my analyst one interpretation in one session, and I was myself again."

"My sudden fear of AIDS is totally irrational, and getting information about it has not helped. Even though there's no way I've been exposed, I think about it all the time. I'm going back to therapy to find out what my anxiety is all about."

"In my three years of therapy, I was able to calm my fears about commitment and get married. During my wife's pregnancy, two years after therapy ended, I started to become very anxious and had recurrent nightmares about a newcomer in town who's trying to kill me. I returned to therapy to work on what it means to me to be a father—an issue that never came up before."

◆ Task 2 ◆
Explore Other Routes to
Emotional Well-Being

Good psychotherapy is an exciting, life-enhancing experience. It increases your creativity and your sense of what is possible. There are many ways to maintain the benefits of therapy and cope with new problems. You can find existing opportunities for exploration, self-expression, problem solving, and growth similar to those that therapy provided or you can create such situations yourself. Consider these other routes to emotional well-being.

• *Talk to someone you trust.* Some people are natural, intuitive helpers. Talk things over with a wise friend, a relative, or a spiritual adviser who can offer you a good ear and some gentle advice. You can also put together a support group of people in circumstances similar to your own. Simply sharing a difficulty with others may help.

You may want to schedule a regular time to talk with a special friend, your partner, or a support group. Set apart the meeting times as you would your therapy time.

• *Make changes in your life-style.* Time away from stressful activities or simply breaks from routine are refreshing and restore our depleted resources.

We can make an important contribution to our well-being by eating and sleeping well and exercising. If your body is tired, starving, or jolted with overdoses of sugar, caffeine, or tobacco, eventually you will feel bad. Exercise works in a number of ways. It provides a sense of accomplishment while calming and relaxing us. You look and feel better if you exercise.

• *Create meaningful opportunities.* Below is a list of activities that can provide some of what you used to have in therapy.

• *Take special care of yourself on a regular basis.* Be generous with yourself and make time for activities that are nurturing and gratifying. Treat yourself to something special from time to time.

• *Learn your family history.* Talk to relatives and reconstruct your family history. Notice repetitions of themes from generation to generation. Make a genogram (diagram of your family history), and write down your findings for the next generation.

• *Keep a dream log.* Regularly record your dreams to help you understand your inner life more deeply. Think about them in the way you learned in your therapy.

If this is a new area for you, consider keeping the dream log in the following way. Write your thoughts and feelings about the location and characters in each dream, and see whether they remind you of yourself, anyone in your adult life, or someone from your childhood. Try to locate and understand any themes in your dreams.

Or make a list of the animate and inanimate objects in your dream. With the understanding that each element in your dream is your creation and represents some part of yourself, choose any object and describe who you are and the function you serve. For example, you might choose to write a monologue from the point of view of a dog that appears in a dream. You would say: "I am the dog in _____'s dream. I am playful and long for attention. I am always looking for someone to care for me." To learn more about dreams, see "Resources," page 250.

• *Develop and pursue new interests.* Participate in athletics, or take a course in something you have always wanted to learn. You might find meditation, movement, or dance therapy rewarding and helpful in reducing stress.

• *Volunteer.* On a regular basis, give something of yourself to an organization or cause that is meaningful to you.

• *Join a self-help group.* Self-help groups provide therapeutic experiences for people with similar problems and often have good records of success. Group members focus on a particular theme or problem, share experiences, and offer one another support. There is a self-help or support group for nearly every kind of issue; check "Resources," page 238, for some examples. Local Y's and church groups offer workshops on various subjects and may also house self-help groups.

• *Get special training, counseling, or planning assistance.* A number of programs offer training or counseling in such areas as managing stress (relaxation training, yoga, hypnosis), becoming more assertive, financial management, selecting a career, or making the most of retirement.

• *Keep a journal.* Throughout this book you have been encouraged to record your thoughts and feelings. Continuing the journal is a particularly good way to keep building on the gains that you have made in therapy. A journal provides a private and safe way to express and explore your thoughts and feelings. Writing down experiences, dreams, and fantasies promotes understanding and provides an opportunity to plan, keep track of your progress, and gain perspective.

◆ **Read books and articles.**   Many popular self-help books are written by thoughtful experts who share their insights and experience. Reading can provide new ideas, inspiration, and reassuring information.

An annotated bibliography of helpful books on a variety of topics can be found in the Resources section of this book.

◆ Task 3 ◆
Continue Using This Book

Although this book is not a replacement for therapy, it is here as a resource for you for as long as you need it. Rereading of relevant pages can act as a refresher course, reminding you of what you once knew.

Refer to the text for specific help, or use your handwritten responses to remember what it was like when you were in therapy. Pay special attention to those tasks that were particularly helpful the first time around. Here are some ideas of how you can continue using this book:

- *For help in understanding or managing a current problem.* Remember to use the Tools for Success: Curiosity, Powers of Observation, Empathy, Receptivity, and Clear Communication —pages 137–148.
- *If you cannot figure out what is bothering you.*   Take stock, Chapter 1 to pinpoint what may be troubling you. Reread Task 2 in Chapter 7 on overcoming obstacles to change. Note if you are restricting yourself with self-defeating beliefs. Reading page 126 will help you set priorities to reduce your distress.
- *If you are having a hard time in a relationship.*   Check the sections on building a relationship with your therapist, pages 79 and 116. See what lessons you can apply to your current relationship.
- *To facilitate decision making if your problems are getting too much for you to handle on your own.*   Read Chapter 2 to help you decide whether to return to therapy.
- *If you are getting ready to make a leap forward.*   Reread the quotes throughout the book. Someone may have said something that strikes a chord.

By giving yourself the kind of care and attention that your therapist accorded you and by using the tools and strategies you learned in therapy, you can handle your daily life well, continue to overcome any problems that emerge, and build on the gains that you made.

This book has helped you to become an active, aware participant in the therapy process. By helping you master a series of tasks and by teaching you to be aware of what works for you and what does not, it enabled you to learn and grow.

You have seen that by breaking down a large task into small steps, you can accomplish a lot. You could walk across the entire country by taking one step at a time. Don't stop now. Continue your journey of self-exploration and growth throughout your life.

•Appendix•
When Someone You
Care About Needs Help

♦ How to Tell Someone That You Think
He or She Needs Help ♦

It is hard to see someone we care about in distress. We want to help, but often we don't know what to do or are afraid that we might make things worse. This chapter focuses on how to decide if someone has a problem best addressed by therapy, and how you can be effective in seeing that he or she gets help.

The next exercises help you put your finger on what is troubling you about the person.

I think _____ **may need therapy because he or she**

_____ is doing badly at work or school.
_____ is talking about suicide.

_____ is a danger to others.

_____ is coping poorly with a difficult life circumstance.

_____ is having trouble thinking clearly.

_____ is self-defeating.

_____ is threatening others with harm.

_____ lacks self-confidence.

_____ is violent.

_____ has troublesome relationship(s).

_____ is pessimistic or unrealistic about his or her ability to cope.

_____ is abusing drugs, alcohol, or food.

_____ is (sad) (angry) (anxious) (distressed) (agitated) (out of control) (panicked) (dissatisfied).

_____ complains about the same problems without doing anything about them.

_____ keeps getting into the same messy situations, without any idea of how to avoid or resolve them.

_____ feels awful about him / herself.

_____ has sudden mood swings.

_____ wants to change.

_____ has sleep difficulties.

_____ can't get along with friends.

_____ keeps getting into trouble with authorities.

_____ wants help.

_____ or, _____

Since none of us is perfect, it can be very uncomfortable to tell someone that you think he or she needs help. You may worry that your friend or family member will be embarrassed or angry or will blame you as the bearer of unwelcome news. Nevertheless, taking a chance and expressing your concern may be a turning point, providing the push the person needs to get help. Here are some guidelines to help you think about what to say and how to say it.

Guidelines for a Caring Confrontation

• **Be direct.**   Even if your loved one reacts defensively at first, talk directly about the problem you see. Direct communication invites serious consideration; indirect approaches can confuse, frighten, and isolate your loved one.

• *Know how you feel about the person and his or her problem.* You may feel concerned, worried, pained, upset, frightened, anxious, saddened, or angered when you see your loved one suffering. Be aware of what you feel before initiating this caring confrontation. Even a person in serious trouble may resist constructive advice if he or she senses that you have your own ax to grind. Often, if you tell someone how you feel first, he or she will be more receptive to the rest of your message.

• *Speak in a way that is caring, concerned, and nonjudgmental.* People will react to both your manner and the content of what you have to say. If your manner is critical, it will be distracting to your listener and cloud the intent of your communication. Let the person know that you care. (Read page 146 for help in communicating skillfully.)

• *Build on areas of agreement.* If the person experiences the problem too, ask what he or she wants to do to deal with it. If the person is at a loss, this is a good time to suggest therapy. You might give him or her this book, pointing out Chapter 1, "Taking Stock," and Chapter 2, "Choosing Therapy."

• *Discuss the benefits of therapy.* If therapy has worked for you or others you know, share these experiences. It is encouraging and reassuring to know that other people have been in the same boat and that there is effective help available.

• *Know when to back off.* Accord your family member or friend the right to differ. Often it takes time for someone to respond to this sort of gentle confrontation. Give him or her time to think things over. If you wish to persist, continue at another time. Unless he or she is in serious difficulty or is your dependent, there is little more that you can do.

• *Know when to persist.* Do not give up if your family member or friend is abusing drugs or alcohol, exhibits a severe disturbance, or is engaged in life-threatening behavior (see page 22). Speaking up under these circumstances may be especially difficult, but don't back off. Get support from others. Things will seldom get better by themselves. Many hot lines (see "Resources," page 237) will advise you on how to get help for people in just these circumstances. Here are some examples of caring confrontations:

◆

"I have noticed that you seem very unhappy lately. You are tearful in the morning and don't eat much at lunch-time. It makes me sad to see you this way."

"When you say that life is not worth living, I get very frightened for you. I really want you to go to therapy to get some help."

"I feel bad for you when I hear about another disappointing relationship. Maybe someone could help you figure out what keeps going wrong."

"You seem to be having so much unhappiness in your marriage and seem so confused about what to do about it. I'm sad to see you this way."

◆

It is important to let the person know that you care, tell him or her what you observe and what you feel about it. It is a good idea to plan what you will say. Using the guidelines for a caring confrontation, the next exercise can help you anticipate and practice the conversation.

What I could say to this person?

Put yourself in the other's shoes and imagine how you would feel hearing a certain message. Do you want to adjust what you will say?

What Else to Try

If your caring confrontation did not work and the problem persists, there are several other options to consider:

• Involve concerned friends or family members and work together to develop a plan of action.

- If the person is important to you or the problem is affecting you too, schedule a consultation with a psychotherapist for yourself. Your own sessions can provide you with some understanding of the person's problem, relief from your own worry, and suggestions about what else you might consider.
- If the person is a substance abuser, contact the local chapter of an appropriate self-help group and attend meetings for friends and relatives of abusers. (See "Resources," page 239.)
- If the person is engaged in destructive behavior or experiences severe disturbance (see page 247), consult a psychiatrist to see whether medication or hospitalization might be appropriate. A psychiatrist who thinks either is advisable will suggest next steps.
- Read books (see "Resources," page 228), attend workshops, and speak to others who have had the problem. Become knowledgeable about the particular problem and learn about all possible avenues of help. If your loved one refuses to take the problem seriously, you may find it useful to learn what others have found effective in dealing with someone who is denying an important problem.

◆ Does Your Child Need Therapy? ◆

There are many reasons why it is difficult to know when one's child may need therapy. A child's capacity to talk about problems is limited. Children communicate indirectly, through their activities; their eating, sleeping, learning, and playing will often provide the clues to any distress. In fact, since it is so rare for a child to ask directly for professional help, give such a request serious consideration.

It is hard to be objective about your own child's emotional state. On the one hand, if we tend to blame ourselves for whatever happens to our children, we may not want to see real problems that need to be addressed.

On the other hand, we may mistakenly interpret minor problems as a signal for psychotherapy rather than as a normal part of growing up.

Although parents and family members do play a part in children's emotional distress, there are many other influences on a child as well. Children are born with a certain constitution into a particular culture and have many experiences that are beyond the control of their families.

We need to evaluate any psychological problem our child has according to his or her age. For example, it is not out of the ordinary for a five-year-old to cry and cling to his mother the first days of school. Yet a child three years older who expresses the same behavior is probably in psychological trouble. The rebelliousness, anger, and heightened resistance to parental authority found in the adolescent or the two-year-old is not appropriate behavior for the second grader.

The Child Symptom Checklist below can help you figure out whether your young child or teenager could use professional help. Complete the exercise according to your child's age. The entire checklist should be filled out if your child is a teenager. There are guidelines for interpreting your responses at the end of the checklist.

CHILD SYMPTOM CHECKLIST

My child

_____ has little energy, is listless, apathetic, lacks curiosity.*

_____ is sad.

_____ is irritable.†

_____ is not gaining enough weight, according to the pediatrician.

_____ bangs his or her head.*

_____ doesn't sleep well (sleeps fitfully, has nightmares, awakens frequently).

_____ is not close to any adult.*

Continue the chart if the child is over 1½. (You have finished the chart if the child is under 1½.)

_____ is tense or apprehensive.

_____ is cruel to animals.*

_____ eats nonfood items.*

_____ has stomachaches, headaches.

_____ has night terrors, with sweating, rapid breathing and heartbeat.

Continue the chart if your child is over 4. (You have finished the chart if your child is 4 or under.)

_____ is clingy.†

_____ has no interest in playing with other children.*

_____ avoids with anxiety: high places, outdoors, elevators, dirt, school, animals, being separated from parent.*

_____ is excessively neat, orderly, and conforming.†

_____ has insomnia.
_____ is unable to speak so that he or she can be understood.*
_____ eats too much or too little.

Continue the chart if your child is over 6. (You have finished the chart if your child is 6 or under.)
_____ masturbates publicly.
_____ stutters, twitches, wets or soils bed, sucks thumb.
_____ is obstinate.†
_____ exhibits him- or herself sexually.
_____ likes to watch others unclothed.
_____ engages in destructive behavior.
_____ is preoccupied with his or her own thoughts and ignores what is going on in the real world.*
_____ is quarrelsome.†
_____ is disobedient.†
_____ sets fires.*
_____ finds reasons not to go to school.
_____ talks about suicide.*
_____ tried to end his or her life.°
_____ has put him- or herself in danger of hurting or killing him- or herself.*
_____ has asked to talk to someone (a professional) about his or her worries, feelings, or some problem.*
_____ stays away from adults or peers.
_____ is unwilling to try new things, convinced he or she cannot accomplish them.†
_____ daydreams a lot.
_____ sleepwalks.
_____ cannot sit still at home or in a larger group setting.
_____ cannot be left by parent.
_____ is fearful.
_____ cries, laughs easily.
_____ sees or hears things not there.*
_____ is failing or marginally passing in school.

Continue the chart if your child is over 9. (You have finished the chart if your child is 9 or under.)
_____ has run away from home overnight.
_____ is truant.
_____ uses drugs or alcohol.
_____ is overweight.
_____ is 15 pounds underweight.*
_____ is not seen eating.*
_____ demonstrates reckless behavior.
_____ is confused about his or her sexual identity.

The starred (*) items are symptoms to take very seriously. If your child exhibits any of these symptoms, it is important for you to talk with a professional specially trained to understand the emotional needs of children.

The items marked † are character traits that can be difficult to live with, yet do not necessarily require professional attention. You could get a lot from attending workshops or reading books about how to parent more successfully.

If many of these traits are present or if you have checked a number of the items on the list, consider getting professional advice. You can consult a therapist who specializes in children or adolescents, see a family therapist, or obtain psychological testing for your child to see whether therapy for your youngster and/or counseling for you could help.

If a teacher or other professional recommends therapy for your child, give it serious consideration. A thoughtful and caring professional may see something that you miss because you are so closely involved. At the same time, it makes sense to evaluate the situation carefully; even a well-meaning professional can be mistaken. If you are uncertain, a second opinion from the school psychologist or an outside therapist can give you additional information.

◆

"When I was eight my parents split up. My parents fought anytime they had anything to do with each other. That year my doctor told my mother that I had gained ten pounds. By the time I was eleven, I was forty pounds overweight. No one took it seriously; even my pediatrician would tease me about my love of food. I wish that I had gotten some help. Instead of dealing with my upset over my parents' divorce, I stuffed myself."

"I don't remember much of the therapy I had in fifth grade. I know I saw the doctor for almost a year and stopped being terrified of going to school."

◆

Your teenager might want to review the self-check list below. It is designed to highlight the particular worries that most commonly bring teenagers into therapy. Your teenager may also want to read Chapters 1 and 2 to assess his or her own need for therapy.

Check the category that most accurately describes how often the following statements are true for you.

TEEN SELF-CHECK SYMPTOM LIST

Never	Sometimes	Frequently	
☐	☐	☐	I am unable to do schoolwork.
☐	☐	☐	I believe that no one likes me.
☐	☐	☐	I feel bad about myself.
☐	☐	☐	I abuse drugs or alcohol.*
☐	☐	☐	I have tried to hurt myself.*
☐	☐	☐	My sexual activity is without pleasure.
☐	☐	☐	I am not in control of my sexual activity.
☐	☐	☐	I forget to use birth control.*
☐	☐	☐	I am confused about my sexual orientation.
☐	☐	☐	I go on eating binges.
☐	☐	☐	I make myself vomit after I eat.*
☐	☐	☐	I do not want to eat.
☐	☐	☐	I have trouble sleeping.
☐	☐	☐	I have night terrors or nightmares.
☐	☐	☐	I think about killing myself.*
☐	☐	☐	I have missed school for other than medical reasons.
☐	☐	☐	I am depressed.
☐	☐	☐	I am confused.
☐	☐	☐	Things seem unreal or bizarre.*
☐	☐	☐	I see things or hear things that are not there.*
☐	☐	☐	I feel hopeless.
☐	☐	☐	I am afraid I am going crazy.
☐	☐	☐	I have run away from home overnight.*
☐	☐	☐	I am unable to make friends.
☐	☐	☐	I am failing or marginally passing in school.

If you have answered *Frequently* to any of the statements above, a therapist can be very useful to you. If you have answered *Sometimes* to any of the starred (*) items, you need to see a therapist as soon as you can. Your parents, doctor, school guidance counselor, or religious adviser can direct you to a therapist. There is help, and the sooner you connect with it, the sooner you will be feeling and doing better.

◆

"When I was fifteen I thought I was crazy. I worried a lot and couldn't concentrate at school. One day I overheard an older girl

talking about a clinic where she talked to someone about an upsetting dream. I knew that my thoughts and feelings were the same kind of crazy as her dream. I made up my mind to get my parents to take me to that clinic. I began acting out my idea of crazy, moaning and sighing a lot and being mysterious about it when my parents asked what was wrong. They became worried and agreed to take me to the clinic. I was grateful that they didn't press me too much about why I wanted to go. Even though the clinic was quite a distance from home, they took me and had their own meetings with a social worker.

"I was very scared during the first interview. I was torn between my fear of exposing how crazy I was and my eagerness to be accepted as a patient. I didn't know how strange to act. Somehow I was accepted, and I came to see a nice, understanding doctor every week for a year and a half until I went away to college."

◆

The Kinds of Professional Help Available

Whatever kind of therapy you choose for your child, be sure that the therapist is specially trained and experienced with that age group. If your child is young, be sure to look for a trained child therapist who will also work actively with you. If your child is an adolescent, choose someone experienced in working with teens and their special problems.

Individual therapy. A child therapist can see your child one or more times a week. The therapist and your child may talk and engage in play activities especially designed to bring out and work through the troubles your child experiences.

When your child is in therapy, your cooperation and involvement are important. Most likely, if your child is twelve or under, you will have the opportunity to meet with the child's therapist or a different therapist in your child's behalf. The therapist will use your feedback to further your child's treatment, will try to help you understand your child in a different way, and will suggest what you can do to help your child progress.

Although you may learn how your child is doing generally, it is unlikely that the child therapist will share the specifics of what happens in the sessions. A therapist often makes an agreement with a youngster that what occurs in the sessions will be kept confidential. This makes self-expression safe for your child, while helping him or her to trust the therapist's loyalty. The exception to this rule of confidentiality occurs if the therapist is seriously concerned about your child's welfare.

Counseling for parents. If you feel confused or out of control as a parent, you and your co-parent can see a professional on your child's behalf. Counseling can help you understand the challenges and stresses of children in your child's age group, while providing you with the guidance you need to be helpful.

Family therapy. You can work with a family therapist, who will mobilize the resources of your entire family to help resolve your child's difficulties. Family therapists believe that adjustments in family relationships are more likely to help small children with problems than is therapy for the child alone or counseling for parents. Family sessions that include everyone or one or both parents are sometimes more acceptable to a teenager uncomfortable with the idea of therapy. The family members can work on improving the family dynamics and any contribution they make to the problem. Sometimes, after family sessions, teenagers decide to continue with their own individual therapy.

Evaluating Your Child's Therapy

In most cases, it is not up to us to evaluate another person's therapy. However, since it is our responsibility to find the best resource and look out for our children, we need to be reasonably sure that therapy is helping.

If your child goes willingly to sessions and the disturbing symptoms have lessened, chances are the therapy is proceeding well and needs to continue.

You may think that your child is doing well enough and that therapy is no longer needed. Just as clients think about leaving therapy when the going gets rough or when things are going well for the moment, you may be tempted to take your child out of therapy before he or she is really ready. Before ending your child's therapy, discuss your decision fully with the therapist to be sure that you are doing the best for your child.

You may be uncertain about what to do if your child is getting worse or is protesting going to therapy. There may be times in therapy when your child is working on feelings that are difficult to manage. Since it's especially hard for children to talk about their worries, these feelings may be expressed in difficult behavior at home or in school. It can look as if your child is getting worse, yet the increased difficulty rarely lasts for long. See what explanation the therapist offers, and seek a consultation if you continue to be concerned. (See page 166 for more information about obtaining a consultation.) Not unlike adults in therapy, children who have initially found relief in expressing themselves in therapy may become reluctant to continue when faced with difficult or uncomfortable material. (Reread page 120, about adults' experiences when there are hard times in therapy.)

Other children, usually seven and older, may feel stigmatized by going to therapy and worry that their peers will disapprove. These children may go through the motions of protesting even while they feel better seeing the therapist. Your child probably needs his protests to protect his pride.

Pride is rarely the issue for the nursery-school-aged child. If your very young child cries and protests going to therapy, there are a few possible explanations. Your child may have trouble leaving you, or the therapist may be going too quickly or may not be in tune with what is going on with your child. See what the therapist has to say.

It is hard to know when to insist that a child continue therapy. Speak with your child and see if you can understand the reasons he or she doesn't want to go to sessions. Engage in a conversation without promising to stop the therapy or insisting that your child continue. Then schedule some time to speak with the therapist.

If the need for therapy persists, and you are reasonably sure that the therapist is warm, competent, and knowledgeable about your child, do insist that the child continue. Your child may need you to take the responsibility for his or her continuing in therapy.

Teenagers either seldom mention their therapy or protest going. Since teenagers do well in therapy when it is their own choice, insisting on their continuing is rarely recommended. If the teen translates his protests into action and hasn't gone to therapy for a protracted period of time, take it seriously. Respecting your teenager's need for independence, you may want to agree that he or she can stop and suggest that there may be a future time when he or she may want to return to therapy.

Often a therapist will agree that stopping for now makes the most sense. Teenagers do come and go in therapy. However, therapists sometimes recommend that the teen continue because of serious problems.

Dangerous behavior and serious symptoms (see starred items, page 219) are the exception to the rule of not insisting that an adolescent remain in therapy. After a thoughtful process with everyone involved, you can give your teenager the choice of staying with his or her current therapist or changing to someone else. However, you do need to insist that the teen stay in therapy until the serious problems are no longer a concern.

◆ Does Your Aging Parent Need Therapy? ◆

Psychotherapy can benefit people of any age. It is often overlooked as a resource for older people, both by therapists, who most often work with younger clients, and by elders, who may think of therapy as being only for "crazy people."

Having an aging parent can be painful under the best of circumstances. Often it is difficult to see our parents as vulnerable and frail rather than as protective, strong, and caring. Unresolved personal and family issues may come to the fore with surprising strength. Old conflicts, long-buried hopes and resentments, as well as new, unfamiliar feelings can present themselves for attention.

When Should You Consider Psychotherapy for Your Parent?

Most elders do well with their lives, considering all they have to manage. They are called upon to deal with the deaths of friends and family, loss of physical strength and youthful beauty, and loss of social roles and status. A certain amount of grieving is natural, expectable, and healthy.

But for some, old age can become a period of real deprivation. Poor health or inadequate social contact, little meaningful activity, or decreased financial resources can overwhelm even those who have coped well in the past. Their understandable upset over adjusting to very real deprivation cannot be addressed by psychotherapy alone. Elders who are deprived need to have their lives enriched and their resources increased in order to experience a sense of well-being.

Psychotherapy may be helpful for those elders who suffer from depression (the most pervasive problem among the elderly), hypochondriasis, confusion and memory loss, anxiety, unwarranted suspiciousness, or psychosis.

Before deciding to try therapy, your parent needs a thorough physical examination conducted by a physician familiar with the aged. Many emotional problems can be caused by physical ailments or reactions to medication.

Since poor nutrition adds to the deterioration of mental functioning, your parent's food intake needs to be evaluated. Some of the drugs your parent is taking may have side effects, which include altered mental states. Alcoholism is a serious problem for the elderly and affects mental functioning. Hearing loss, poor eyesight, and congestive heart failure can cause or add to confusion and depression.

The terror of Alzheimer's and other hopeless conditions can discourage us from obtaining potentially helpful treatment. Yet since half of the mental problems among the elderly are treatable and reversible, the sooner the problem is treated, the sooner there will be a positive result.

What Kind of Therapy Can Be Helpful?

If it is possible, your parent should be seen by a therapist with special training and experience with the aged. Aging is especially complex with biochemical, social, and psychological changes to consider. Many university hospitals have geriatric departments that provide physical and psychological services. If this specialized service is unavailable, be sure to find a compassionate professional who demonstrates an understanding of your parent's situation.

Individual, group, family, or couple therapy can all be appropriate for an elderly client. If your parent resists, don't be discouraged. Be patient and creative. See if a therapist will meet with your parent at home or in a familiar place like a physician's office, senior center, church or synagogue, hospital, or clinic. Accompany your parent to help overcome his or her fear. It can be hard to get started, yet well worth it. See the Resource section for books on how to help your aging parents, page 249.

♦ When Someone You Care About ♦ Needs a Consultation

Most of the time when the person we care about enters therapy, all proceeds without a hitch. We are optimistic that the therapist and our child, our parent, or another family member are working toward solving the problems that worried us. Yet sometimes we may have serious concerns about that person's therapy and may not know what to do.

If you are worried about the therapeutic treatment of your child, your parent, or another family member, do speak to the treating therapist and share all your concerns. The information you provide can increase the therapist's understanding, and he or she can adjust the therapy accordingly. The talk may relieve your concern. Your relative's therapist may not be willing to talk with you in detail about the therapy, which is confidential. He or she will probably listen to your concerns and offer some reassurance as appropriate.

After speaking with the therapist, you may remain uncertain about the benefits of therapy. Seek a consultation with another therapist if:

- The person you care about has been getting worse for a protracted period of time.
- The person is seriously protesting going to sessions, yet seems to need therapy.
- You are unsure whether the person continues to need therapy and do not feel reassured by the therapist.
- The therapist has done something unethical, unprofessional, or hurtful (see page 162).

You can ask the person you care about to accompany you, or you can see the consultant by yourself. (See page 166 on how to prepare for a consultation.) You may learn about other resources or obtain information that will reassure you about your loved one's therapy.

Now you have taken the opportunity to think about someone else who is in distress and have considered how to approach and speak with him or her about your concerns. Even if your interventions have not gone as you'd hoped, you have made an effort to do something caring that may make a difference in the future. If the person has gotten help as the result of your efforts, take a moment to feel good about what you have accomplished.

Resources

Contents

◆ Learning About Therapy ◆

If a book listed in this resource section is not available at your local bookstore or library, you can have your bookseller order it for you or order it directly from the publisher yourself.

GENERAL INFORMATION

Ehrenberg, O., and M. Ehrenberg. *The Psychotherapy Maze: A Consumer's Guide to Getting In and Out of Therapy*, rev. ed. New York: Simon and Schuster, 1986. Especially helpful for the descriptions of the various approaches to therapy.

The National Institute of Mental Health. *Mental Health Directory, 1985.* Superintendent of Documents, U.S. Government Printing Office, Washington, DC 20402-9325; (202) 783-3238. Lists outpatient clinics and inpatient treatment facilities for adults and children nationwide.

The National Mental Health Association, Publications Department, 1021 Prince St., Alexandria, VA 22314-2971; (703) 684-7722. Send for their catalogue, which contains a wide variety of useful listings, including informative, low-cost pamphlets.

Weinberg, G. *The Heart of Psychotherapy.* New York: St. Martin's Press, 1984. The nitty-gritty process of therapy from a therapist's point of view.

INDIVIDUAL THERAPY

Alther, L. *Other Women.* New York: New American Library, 1985. An engaging novel describing the process of therapy from both the therapist's and the client's perspective.

Greenberg, J. *I Never Promised You a Rose Garden.* New York: New American Library, 1977. A moving account of a young woman's recovery from a severe disturbance.

Lindner, R. *The Fifty Minute Hour: A Collection of True Psychoanalytic Tales.* New York: Delta Diamond Library, 1986. Reissue of the classic.

Miller, Alice. *The Drama of the Gifted Child: Prisoners of Childhood.* New York: Basic Books, 1981. Describes poignantly the effects of narcissistic disturbances (problems with the sense of true self).

Rossner, J. *August.* New York: Warner Books, 1984. An engrossing novel about an extraordinary client and her insightful analyst.

FAMILY THERAPY

Napier, A., and C. A. Whitaker. *The Family Crucible.* New York: Bantam, 1980. A vivid description of the actual course of one family's therapy, with theoretical explanations.

Satir, V. *Conjoint Family Therapy.* Palo Alto, CA: Science & Behavior Books, 1967. Describes the special role that communication can play in family therapy.

GROUP THERAPY

Yalom, I. D. *The Theory and Practice of Group Psychotherapy.* New York: Basic Books, 1975. A clear, readable account of the benefits of group therapy.

CHILD THERAPY

Axline, V. *Play Therapy.* New York: Ballantine, 1969. This authoritative and vivid explanation of how psychotherapy helps children develop and grow provides many examples of youngsters in therapy.

Bloch, D. *So the Witch Won't Eat Me.* Boston: Houghton Mifflin, 1979. This child analyst explains the reasons behind children's fear and anger and demonstrates how therapy helps resolve emotional problems.

◆ Professional Organizations ◆

Some of the national professional organizations below will give you the names of qualified members in your local area (national referral service), while others will direct you to their local branches for referrals (referrals to affiliates). You can also locate a therapist by looking at the membership listings of a professional organization (directory or registry). Registries and directories differ; directories list all the members of an organization, while registries list only those members who choose to be included. Thus, many qualified members of an organization may not be included in a registry. You can often find directories or registries in public or university libraries.

When you request a referral, be sure to state any special preferences that you have in a therapist: a specific approach to therapy, experience with a special problem or population, or a focus on individual, group, couple, or family therapy.

CLINICAL PSYCHOLOGISTS
American Psychological Association, 1200 17th St., NW, Washington, DC 20036; (202) 955-7600. Referrals to affiliates, directory.

CLINICAL SOCIAL WORKERS
American Board of Examiners in Clinical Social Work, 8403 Colesville Rd., Suite 340, Silver Spring, MD 20910; (301) 495-4465. Has Directory of Board Certified Clinical Social Workers. National referral service.

National Association of Social Workers, 7981 Eastern Ave., Silver Spring, MD 20910; (301) 565-0333.

National Federation of Societies of Clinical Social Work Psychotherapists, c/o Kenneth L. Adams, 22101 L St., NW, Washington, DC 20037; (202) 223-6134. These organizations jointly publish a *National Registry of Health Providers in Clinical Social Work*. Registry.

COUNSELORS
National Academy of Certified Clinical Mental Health Counselors, 5999 Stevenson Ave., Alexandria, VA 22304; (703) 823-9800. An affiliate of the American Association for Counseling and Development. National referral service, registry.

GROUP THERAPISTS
American Group Psychotherapy Association, 25 East 21st St., New York, NY 10010; (212) 477-2677. National referral service, directory.

MARITAL AND FAMILY THERAPIST (MARRIAGE COUNSELOR)
American Association of Marriage and Family Therapy, 1717 K St., NW, Suite 407, Washington, DC 20006; (202) 429-1825. National referral service, registry.

American Family Therapy Association, 1255 23rd St., NW, Washington, DC 20037; (202) 659-7666. National referral service, directory.

PASTORAL COUNSELORS
American Association of Pastoral Counselors, 9508A Lee Highway, Fairfax, VA 22031; (703) 385-6967. National referral service.

PSYCHIATRIC NURSES
American Nurses Association, 2420 Pershing Rd., Kansas City, MO 64108; (816) 474-5720. Registry.

PSYCHIATRISTS
American Psychiatric Association, 1400 K St., NW, Washington, DC 20005; (202) 682-6000. Referrals to affiliates, directory.

SEX THERAPISTS
American Association of Sex Educators, Counselors, and Therapists, 11 Dupont Circle, NW, Suite 220, Washington, DC 20036-1207; (202) 462-1171. Directory.

◆ Schools of Therapy ◆

Here are selected readings to introduce you to each school of therapy and suggestions about organizations you can contact for more information (literature or booklets) and referrals (referral service; referrals to affiliates). Many of the referral services in this section are informal and depend upon someone on the staff of a program knowing a former trainee or a colleague in your locale. You can also locate a therapist who practices a specific approach through one of the professional organizations listed above.

BEHAVIOR THERAPY
Agras, S. *Panic: Facing Fears, Phobias, and Anxiety.* New York: W. H. Freedman, 1985. Reviews current research and clinical experience and shows how behavior therapy can resolve a variety of phobias, panic attacks, and anxieties.

Rathus, S. A., and J. S. Nevid. *Behavior Therapy: Strategies for Solving Problems in Living.* New York: Signet, 1977. Applications to phobias, sexual dysfunction, overeating, insomnia, anxiety, nonassertive and other self-defeating behavior.

Patterson, G. R. *Families: Applications of Social Learning to Family Life.* Champaign, IL: Research Press, 1975. Straightforward, clear, and useful application of social learning theory to family life.

◆

Association for the Advancement of Behavior Therapy, 15 West 36th St., New York, NY 10018; (212) 279-7970. Directory.

BODY THERAPIES (BIOENERGETICS, CORE ENERGETICS, AND RADIX)
Boadella, D. *Wilhelm Reich: The Evolution of His Work.* Boston: Arkana, 1985. A detailed account of the development of the concepts that underlie many current approaches to body therapy.

Kurtz, R., and H. Prestera. *The Body Reveals: What Your Body Says About You.* New York: Harper & Row, 1984. Clear and enjoyable illustrated descriptions of what different body types show about character structure.

Lowen, A. *Bioenergetics.* New York: Penguin, 1986. A reissue of the original, introductory book on bioenergetics details basics of this approach. By the same author: *Narcissism: Denial of the True Self.*

Smith, E. W. L. *The Body in Psychotherapy.* Jefferson, NC: McFarland and Company (Box 611, Jefferson, NC 28640; $20 plus postage and handling), 1985. An excellent overview of body therapy from a Radix perspective.

◆

Institute of Core Energetics, 115 East 23rd St., New York, NY 10010; (212) 982-9637 or 505-6767. National referral service, literature.

International Institute for Bioenergetic Analysis, 144 East 36th St., New York, NY 10016; (212) 532-7742. Referrals to affiliates, literature, booklet.

Radix Institute, Route 2, Box 89A, Suite 102, Sery Place, Grandbury, TX 76048; (817) 326-5670. National referral service, literature.

CLIENT-CENTERED THERAPY

Rogers, C. R. *Client-Centered Therapy.* Boston: Houghton Mifflin, 1951. The initial explanation of this approach. By the same author: *On Becoming a Person* and *A Way of Being.*

◆

Center for the Studies of the Person, 1125 Torrey Pines Road, La Jolla, CA 92037; (619) 459-3861. National referral service.

The Association for Humanistic Psychology, 325 Ninth St., San Francisco, CA 94103; (415) 626-2375. Referrals to affiliates.

COGNITIVE THERAPY

Burns, D. *Feeling Good: The New Mood Therapy.* New York: Signet, 1980. Useful exercises to identify and alter the cognitive components of feelings with a focus on depression.

Ellis, A. *Reason and Emotion in Therapy.* New York: Citadel Press, 1962. An exposition of the "rational-emotive" approach, which focuses on altering unproductive and mistaken patterns of thinking that lead to destructive feelings and behavior.

◆

Center for Cognitive Therapy, 133 South 36th St., Room 602, Philadelphia, PA 19104; (215) 898-4100. National referral service.

EXISTENTIAL THERAPY

Bugental, J. *Psychotherapy and Process: The Fundamentals of an Existential-Humanistic Approach.* New York: Random House, 1978. An excellent introduction to existential therapy. By the same author: *The Search for Authenticity: An Existential Approach to Therapy.*

Frankl, V. E. *Man's Search for Meaning: An Introduction to Logotherapy.* New York: Touchstone, 1984. A perspective on existentialism derived from observations of who survived in concentration camps. By the same author: *Psychotherapy and Existentialism: Selected Papers on Logotherapy.*

May, R. *Man's Search for Himself.* New York: Delta, 1953. A humanistic-existential approach. By the same author: *The Discovery of Being: Writings in Existential Psychology* and *Love and Will.* Inspiring discussions of how modern man can attain healthy emotional growth.

◆

Association for Humanistic Psychology. See Client-Centered Therapy.

FAMILY THERAPY (BOWEN-STRUCTURAL, STRATEGIC, STRUCTURAL)

Haley, J. *Uncommon Therapy.* New York: W. W. Norton, 1973. Examples of the intuitive, touching, and sometimes amusing paradoxical interventions made by the master practitioner, Milton Erickson, help to illustrate how strategic therapy works. By the same author: *Leaving Home: The Therapy of Disturbed Young People.*

Minuchin, S. *Family Kaleidoscope.* Cambridge, MA: Harvard University Press, 1984. By the same author: *Families and Family Therapy.* The theory of structural family therapy with illustrative material from actual families.

Papp, P. *The Process of Change.* New York: Guilford Press, 1983. Descriptions of actual family sessions using strategic therapy.

◆

Ackerman Institute for Family Therapy, 149 East 78th St., New York, NY 10021; (212) 879-4900. (Strategic) Referral service.

Family Studies, Inc., 114 East 32nd St., New York, NY 10016; (212) 481-3144. (Structural) Referral service.

Family Therapy Institute of Washington, 5850 Hubbard Dr., Rockville, MD; (301) 984-5730. (Strategic) Referral service.

Georgetown Family Center, 4380 MacArthur Blvd., NW, Washington, DC 20007; (202) 965-0730 (Bowen-Structural) Referral service.

Philadelphia Child Guidance Clinic, Training Dept., 34th and Civic Center Blvd., Philadelphia, PA 19104, (215) 243-2773. (Structural) Referral service.

FEMINIST THERAPY

Gilligan, C. *In a Different Voice: Psychological Theory and Women's Development.* Cambridge, MA: Harvard University Press, 1982. Uses research on the differences in moral development between men and women to show how psychological theories have misunderstood and devalued women.

Greenspan, M. *A New Approach to Women and Therapy.* New York: Mc-

Graw-Hill, 1983. A critique of how conventional therapies—both psycho-analysis and humanistic approaches—have failed women, and a description of a new therapeutic model.

Robbins, J. H., and R. J. Siegel, eds. *Women Changing Therapy: New Assessments, Values, and Strategies in Feminist Therapy.* New York: Harrington Park Press, 1985. A series of essays on such diverse subjects as "The Necessity of Conflict," "Therapists Coping with Sexual Assault," and "The Consequences of Abortion Legislation."

Miller, J. B. *Toward a New Psychology of Women.* Boston: Beacon Press, 1976. A psychoanalyst's inspired description of how women's sense of self has been limited by inequality and how change can take place.

◆

Women's Therapy Centre Institute, 80 East 11th St., Room 101, New York, NY 10003; (212) 420-1974. National referral service.

GESTALT THERAPY

Fagen, J., and I. Shepherd, eds. *Gestalt Therapy Now: Teachings and Applications.* New York: Harper & Row, 1971. A rich collection of articles about the theory, techniques, and applications of Gestalt therapy.

Perls, F., R. Hefferline, and P. Goodman. *Gestalt Therapy.* New York: Julian Press, 1951. The seminal work on this subject introduces the basic concepts.

Polster, E., and M. Polster. *Gestalt Therapy Integrated: Contours of Therapy and Practice.* New York: Vintage, 1974. A sensitive, moving account of how two master practitioners employ Gestalt therapy.

◆

The Gestalt Institute of Cleveland, 1588 Hazel Drive, Cleveland, OH 44106; (216) 421-1700. National referral service.

Association for Humanistic Psychology. See Client-Centered Therapy.

HYPNOTHERAPY

Wolberg, L. R. *Hypnosis: Is It for You?.* New York: Dembner Books, 1982. A balanced, thorough, informative book describing what hypnosis is and how it is used and answering most commonly asked questions on the subject.

◆

American Society of Clinical Hypnosis, 2250 East Devon, Suite 336, Des Plaines, IL 60018; (312) 297-3317. A membership organization for M.D.s, Ph.D. psychologists, and D.D.S.s who use hypnosis in their practice. Send them a self-addressed, stamped business envelope and they will mail you the names of any of their members in your area. National referral service.

Erickson Foundation, 3606 North 24th St., Phoenix, AZ 85016; (602) 956-6196. Referrals to affiliates.

INTERPERSONAL ANALYSIS (SULLIVANIAN, CULTURAL SCHOOL)

Fromm-Reichmann, F. *Principles of Intensive Psychotherapy*. Chicago: University of Chicago Press, 1967. The basic ideas of the interpersonal approach, presented in an accessible way. By the same author: *Psychoanalysis and Psychotherapy*.

◆

William Alanson White Institute of Psychiatry, Psychoanalysis, and Psychology, 20 West 74th St., New York, NY 10023; (212) 873-0725. National referral service.

JUNGIAN ANALYSIS (ANALYTIC PSYCHOLOGY, DEPTH PSYCHOLOGY)

Fordham, F. *An Introduction to Jung's Psychology*. New York: Penguin, 1953. A clear presentation of Jungian ideas and terms.

Hall, C. S., and V. J. Nordby. *A Primer for Jungian Psychology*. New York: New American Library, 1973. A condensation and summary of Carl Jung's life and work.

Jung, C. G. *The Portable Jung*, ed. J. Campbell. New York: Penguin, 1986. Selections from Jung's writings.

Leonard. L. S. *The Wounded Woman: Healing the Father-Daughter Relationship*. Boulder, CO: Shambhala, 1983. A Jungian analyst's readable and understandable look at this subject; illustrates how a Jungian perspective is applied to resolving a specific issue.

◆

C. G. Jung Foundation, 28 East 39th St., New York, NY 10016; (212) 697-6430. They have a book service, (212) 697-6433, with an extensive catalogue. Literature, booklet, referral to affiliates.

NEURO-LINGUISTIC PROGRAMMING

Dilts, R. B., et al. *Neuro-Linguistic Programming I*. Cupertino, CA: Meta Publications, 1979. An introduction to the concepts and theory.

Bandler, R., and J. Grinder. *Frogs into Princes: Neuro-Linguistic Programming*, ed. Steve Andreas. Moab, UT: Real People Press, 1979. Accounts of actual sessions with the principal originators of NLP illustrate how this approach works.

◆

National Association of Neuro-Linguistic Programming, 310 North Alabama, Suite A100, Indianapolis, IN 46204; (317) 636-6059. National referral service.

PSYCHOANALYSIS

Freud, S. *Introductory Lectures on Psychoanalysis.* New York: W. W. Norton, 1977. Also see *Therapy and Technique.* Accessible and readable works by the founder of psychoanalysis.

Greenson, R. R. *The Technique and Practice of Psychoanalysis.* New York: International Universities Press, 1967. This is a clearly written and stimulating account of the basic principals of psychoanalysis written for the professional but accessible to all interested readers.

Kubie, L. *Practical and Theoretical Aspects of Psychoanalysis.* New York: International Univeisities Press, 1975. Written for those considering psychoanalysis.

Reik, T. *Listening with the Third Ear.* New York: Farrar, Straus, 1948. The classic work about the inner experience of the psychoanalyst.

◆

American Psychoanalytic Association, 309 East 49th St., New York, NY 10017; (212) 752-0450. M.D.s only. Booklet, referrals to affiliates.

American Academy of Psychoanalysis, 30 East 40th St., Room 608, New York, NY 10016; (212) 679-4105. M.D.s only. Directory.

National Association for the Advancement of Psychoanalysis, 80 Eighth Ave., Suite 1210, New York, NY 10011; (212) 741-0515. Has member institutions from varied analytic persuasions. Referrals to affiliates, registry.

PSYCHODRAMA

Heisey, M. J. *Clinical Studies in Psychodrama.* Lanham, MD: University Press of America, 1982. The many case examples bring this approach to life.

Moreno, J. L. *The Essential Moreno,* ed. Jonathan Fox. New York: Springer, 1987. A selection from the founder of psychodrama.

Yablonsky, L. *Psychodrama: Resolving Emotional Problems Through Role Playing.* New York: Gardner Press, 1981. Makes clear the many ways psychodrama can be employed.

◆

American Board of Examiners in Psychodrama, Sociometry, and Group Psychotherapy, Box 15572, Washington, DC 20003-0572; (202) 965-4115. National referral service.

SELF PSYCHOLOGY (KOHUTIAN/CHICAGO SCHOOL)

Kohut, H. *How Does Analysis Cure?* Chicago: University of Chicago Press, 1984.

◆

Chicago Institute for Psychoanalysis, 180 North Michigan Ave., Chicago, IL 60601; (312) 726-6300. National referral service.

TRANSACTIONAL ANALYSIS

Berne, E. *Games People Play.* New York: Grove Press, 1964. The book that popularized TA outlines 120 familiar, unproductive patterns of behavior referred to as "games."

Goulding, M. M., and R. Goulding. *Changing Lives Through Redecision Therapy.* New York: Grove Press, 1982. Numerous case examples illustrate how emotional decsions made in childhood can be changed in adult life.

James, M., and D. Jongward. *Born to Win.* Reading, MA: Addison-Wesley, 1971. A workbook that makes the basic concepts of TA come to life as you apply them to yourself.

Steiner, C. *Scripts People Live.* New York: Bantam, 1975. How decisions made in childhood continue to shape adult lives.

◆

International Transactional Analysis Association, 1772 Vallejo Street, San Francisco, CA 94123; (415) 885-5992. Literature, national referral service, referrals to affiliates.

TRANSPERSONAL THERAPY

Mintz, E., and R. Schmeidler. *The Psychic Thread: Paranormal and Transpersonal Aspects of Psychotherapy.* New York: Human Sciences Press, 1983. An excellent overall picture of the transpersonal approach.

Tart, C., ed. *Transpersonal Psychologies,* reissue. San Rafael, CA: Psychological Processes Press [Box 94948, Novato, CA 94901-2510; (415) 883-3530], 1983. A series of essays on this approach.

◆

Association for Humanistic Psychology. See Client-Centered Therapy.

◆ Special Problems and Populations ◆

The following information and resources can help you to understand and cope with special problems. This is only a partial list; no matter what issues you are dealing with, the chances are that you are not alone and that others are thinking and struggling with similar issues. The organizations listed below are intended as suggestions about where to look for help and not as endorsements. You need to use the same care in selecting a support group that you would use in selecting a therapist.

SELF-HELP GROUPS

First, two general references:

National Self-Help Clearing House, 33 West 42nd St., New York, NY 10036; (212) 840-1259. Send a self-addressed, stamped envelope for the name of a specific self-help group in your community and what to look for in a prospective group. The bimonthly newsletter, *The Self-Help Reporter*, published by the Clearing House, costs $10 per year.

Self-Help Source Book: Finding and Forming Self-Help Groups lists and describes many of the self-help groups that exist nationwide. Send $9 to New Jersey Self-Help Clearing House, St. Clare's–Riverside Medical Center, Pocono Rd., Denville, NJ 07834; (201) 625-9565.

Here are more specific suggestions about what to read and whom to contact for a variety of problems and special populations.

ADOPTION: ADULT ADOPTEES / PLANNING FOR ADOPTION / PARENTING ISSUES

Gilman, L. *The Adoption Resource Book*, rev. ed. New York: Harper & Row, 1987. A comprehensive guide to arranging for and completing a successful adoption, with an extensive list of adoption agencies and recommended readings.

Lifton, B. J. *Lost and Found: The Adoption Experience.* New York: Harper & Row, 1988. Reissue of a helpful book that focuses on the psychological and emotional issues of adult adoptees.

Melina, L. R. *Raising Adopted Children: A Manual for Adoptive Parents.* New York: Harper & Row, 1986. Covers all aspects of adoptive parenting.

♦

Adoptees Liberty Movement Association, Box 154, Washington Bridge Station, New York, NY 10033; (212) 581-1568. Self-help group that maintains an international reunion directory of over half a million persons for possible matching between offspring and birth parents.

North American Council on Adoptable Children, 1821 University Ave. W., Suite 275 South, St. Paul, MN 55104; (612) 644-3036. Listing of support groups nationwide for those looking to adopt or parents who have adopted.

Ours, 3307 Highway 100 North, Minneapolis, MN 55422; 24 Hour Helpline (612) 434-4930. National membership organization of adoptive families offering information and problem solving assistance to adoptive families. Referrals to adoption support groups, resource material, and a bimonthly newsletter.

Resolve, Inc., 5 Water St., Arlington, MA 02174; (617) 643-2424. Information and support groups for infertile couples throughout the country.

CHEMICAL DEPENDENCY: ALCOHOLICS / DRUG ABUSERS / FAMILIES / ADULT CHILDREN OF ALCOHOLICS

To obtain extensive catalogues describing the wide range of literature on all aspects of chemical dependency (and other addictions, like compulsive gambling, eating disorders, sexual addiction, and addictive relationships), contact CompCare Publications, (800) 328-3330; in Minnesota, call collect, (612) 559-4800. Hazelden Educational Materials, (800) 328-9000; in Minnesota, (800) 257-0070; in Alaska and outside the USA, (612) 257-4010. Health Communications, (800) 851-9100, or Johnson Institute, (800) 231-5165; in Minnesota, (800) 247-0480.

Black, C. *It Will Never Happen to Me: Children of Alcoholics.* Denver: MAC publishing (1850 High St., Denver, CO), 1981. The first major book on this subject remains an excellent resource for understanding the lifelong impact of growing up in a family with an alcoholic parent and offers the hope of overcoming the problems of Adult Children of Alcoholics (ACoA).

Changes. 1721 Blout Rd., Suite 1, Pompano Beach, FL 33069. Published bimonthly by U.S. Journal of Drug and Alcohol Dependence. Articles by and about ACoA.

Johnson, V. *Intervention: How to Help Someone Who Doesn't Want Help. A Step by Step Guide for Families and Friends of Chemically Dependent Persons.* Minneapolis: Johnson Institute, 1987. By the same author: *I'll Quit Tomorrow.*

Marlin, E. *Hope: New Choices and Recovery Strategies for Adult Children of Alcoholics.* New York: Harper & Row, 1987. Comprehensive and compassionate guideposts for recovery.

Pursch, J. A. *Dear Doc: The Noted Authority Answers Your Questions on Drinking and Drugs.* Minneapolis: CompCare Publications, 1985. An excellent resource for anyone interested in understanding chemical dependency.

Wegsheider, S. *Another Change: Hope and Health for Alcoholic Families.* Palo Alto, CA: Science & Behavior Books, 1980.

Toll-free hot lines for information and referrals:

Alcohol and Drug Counseling, (800) ALCOHOL (24 hours). Counseling, information, and referral.

Drug Abuse, (800) 662-HELP. Referrals to treatment facilities, programs, and self-help groups. National Institute on Drug Abuse.

(800) COCAINE (24 hours). Information about cocaine addiction, treatment.

(800) 554-KIDS; in Maryland, (301) 585-KIDS (M–F, 9–5). Referrals to parent support groups, drug and alcohol treatment centers; educational material. National Federation of Parents for a Drug Free Youth.

(800) 241-7946 (M–F, 8:30–5). Information, referrals, help starting youth or parent groups. National Parents Resource Institute for Drug Education, Inc.

◆

Alcoholics Anonymous (AA), Box 459, Grand Central Station, New York, NY 10163; (212) 696-1100; TDD for the hearing impaired, (212) 686-5454. AA, probably the most successful, long-lived self-help group, has assisted millions in becoming sober. Their twelve-step program has been adopted by numerous other self-help groups.

Al-Anon Family Group Headquarters, Box 862, Midtown Station, New York, NY 10018-0862; (212) 302-7240. Includes information on Alateen. For families and children of alcoholics.

Narcotics Anonymous, Box 9999, Van Nuys, CA 91409; (818) 780-3951. NAR-ANON FAMILY GROUPS, Box 2562, Palos Verdes, CA 90274; (213) 547-5800. Self-help programs set up on the AA model.

Adult Children of Alcoholics, Central Service Board, Box 3216, Torrance, CA 90505; (213) 534-1815. Self-help groups for ACoA.

Children of Alcoholics Foundation, 200 Park Ave., 31st Floor, New York, NY 10166; (212) 351-2680. Resources for children, youth, adults, and health care professionals. Information, publications, and referrals nationwide.

National Association for the Children of Alcoholics, 31582 Coast Highway, Suite B, South Laguna, CA 92677; (714) 499-3889. Clearinghouse for the distribution of information, advocacy, referrals for services, and professional training.

DOMESTIC AND SEXUAL VIOLENCE: DOMESTIC VIOLENCE / SURVIVORS OF CHILD SEXUAL ABUSE / CHILD ABUSE / RAPE

Domestic Violence

Martin, D. *Battered Wives*, rev. ed. San Francisco: Volcano Press (330 Ellis St., San Francisco, CA 94102), 1981. A basic book that shows the context of domestic violence and the legal and social problems faced when women leave abusive spouses.

NiCarthy, G. *Getting Free: A Handbook for Women in Abusive Relationships.* rev. ed. Seattle: Seal Press (Box 13, Seattle, WA 98111), 1986. A guide that helps a woman to think about her own situation, to define abuse (emotional as well as physical), and to consider what she needs to do to change it. Write for Seal Press's excellent reading list on the subject of domestic violence.

Sonkin, D. J., and M. Durphy. *Learning to Live Without Violence: A Handbook for Men.* San Francisco: Volcano Press, 1982. Clear, practical help for men in understanding and taking control of abusive behavior.

Walker, L. *The Battered Woman.* New York: Harper & Row, 1979. While the theory of learned helplessness presented in this book is not empowering because it overlooks the many women who do struggle to free themselves, the book offers an excellent overview of how battering comes to be and how to get out of the destructive situation.

♦

Batterers Anonymous, B. A. Press, 1269 North "E" St., San Bernardino, CA 92405. Call Dr. Jerry Goffman, (714) 884-6809. Self-help program for men who want to control anger and eliminate abusive behavior.

National Coalition Against Domestic Violence, Box 15127, Washington, DC 20003-0127. 24-hour toll-free hot line for referral, information, and support for battered women: (800) 333-SAFE.

Survivors of Child Sexual Abuse

Bass, E., And L. Davis. *The Courage to Heal: A Guide for Women Survivors of Child Sexual Abuse.* New York: Harper & Row, 1988. A compassionate, comprehensive guide to recovery. Full of practical help and inspiring first-person examples. Contains an excellent resource section.

Bass, E., and L. Thornton, eds. *I Never Told Anyone: Writings by Women Survivors of Child Sexual Abuse.* New York: Harper & Row, 1983. Women tell their own painful and moving stories.

Butler, S. *Conspiracy of Silence: The Trauma of Incest.* San Francisco: Volcano Press (330 Ellis St., San Francisco, CA 94102), 1985. A revised edition of one of the original books that show the dimensions of the problem of child sexual abuse from a feminist perspective; still relevant today.

♦

Incest Survivors Anonymous, Box 5613, Long Beach, CA 90805-0613; (213) 428-5599.

Incest Survivor Information Exchange, Box 3399, New Haven, CT 06515. Their newsletter provides a forum where female and male incest survivors can publish their thoughts, writings, and artwork and can form networks. Sample issue $1; yearly rates, $5 bulk mail or $7 first class (free if the price is prohibitive).

Parents United. For parents whose partners (or who themselves) have been sexually involved with children. Adults Molested as Children United. For adults who were molested as children. Daughters and Sons United (Box 952, San Jose, CA 95108; (408) 280-5055). For incest victims and siblings. The groups vary considerably; some are run by professionals and others are self-help groups. Because the model is one of family reconciliation, the groups are not useful for everyone; perpetrators may not be confronted sufficiently, and victims' anger may not receive enough recognition and support.

V.O.I.C.E.S. (Victims of Incest Can Emerge as Survivors), Box 148309, Chicago, IL 60614; (312) 327-1500. A national network providing emotional support for victims and community education.

Child Abuse, Physical and Sexual

Byerly, C. M. *The Mother's Book: How to Survive the Incest of Your Child.* Dubuque, IA: Kendall / Hunt, 1985. A short guide to help mothers with the practical and emotional aspects of their own and their children's recovery. Good resource section.

Colao, F., and T. Hosansky. *Your Children Should Know.* New York: Harper & Row, 1987. How to help your children to protect themselves from sexual abuse and what to do if it occurs.

Herbruck, C. C. *Breaking the Cycle of Child Abuse.* Minneapolis: Winston Press, 1979. A book that looks at both the pain of child abuse and the possibilities for getting help from Parents Anonymous.

Miller, A. *Thou Shall Not Be Aware: Society's Betrayal of the Child.* New York: New American Library, 1986. Uses a psychoanalytic framework to discuss the roots of the victimization of children. By the same author: *For Your Own Good: Hidden Cruelty in Child-Rearing and the Roots of Violence.*

◆

Parents Anonymous, 6733 South Sepulveda Blvd., Suite 270, Los Angeles, CA 90045; (800) 421-0353; in California, (800) 352-0386. Self-help group for parents who want to stop physically abusing their children; offers counseling on the phone plus referrals to state chapters, which will supply information abuot local group meetings.

Child Help National Child Abuse Hotline (800) 422-4453; 24 hour crisis counseling; referrals.

Rape

Adams, C., and J. Fay. *Nobody Told Me It Was Rape: A Parent's Guide to Talking with Teenagers About Acquaintance Rape and Sexual Exploitation.* Santa Cruz, CA; Network Publications, 1984. A brief, to-the-point guidebook.

Brownmiller, S. *Against Our Will.* New York: Bantam, 1976. Places the issue of rape in a political and social context.

Ledray, L. *Recovering from Rape.* New York: Holt, 1986. Very useful emotional support and practical guidance, especially in dealing with the immediate aftermath of being raped: the trauma, the police, the hospital, and the legal system. Has listings of resources in each state.

DISABILITIES

Browne, S., D. Conners, and N. Stern. *With the Power of Each Breath: A Disabled Women's Anthology.* San Francisco: Clies Press (Box 14684, San Francisco, CA 94114), 1985.

Hale, G., ed. *The Source Book for the Disabled.* New York: Bantam, 1981. A guide to all aspects of living with a disability with an emphasis on resources.

Miller, V. *Despite This Flesh: The Disabled in Stories and Poems.* Austin: University of Texas Press (Box 7819, Austin, TX 78713), 1985. A very moving anthology of poetry and stories by disabled men and women.

Weiner, F. *No Apologies: A Guide to Living with a Disability.* New York: St. Martin's Press, 1986. Brief interviews with people with disabilities, families, friends, and professionals, on a variety of topics like living with a disability, sex and education, plus many useful resources and suggested readings.

DIVORCE

Calgrove, M., H. Bloomfield, and P. McWilliams. *How to Survive a Loss.* New York: Bantam, 1981. Brief, to-the-point suggestions about what you can do to get over a loss and move on.

Edwards, M., and E. Hoover. *The Challenge of Being Single: For Divorced, Widowed, Separated and Never Married Men and Women.* New York: Signet, 1974. Positive advice and support for the long-term adjustment to being single again.

Gardner, R. *The Boys and Girls Book About Divorce.* New York: Bantam, 1970. By the same author, *The Boys and Girls Book About Step-families.* Two constructive and reassuring books written for children and of special interest to parents and stepparents.

Krantzler, M. *Creative Divorce: A New Opportunity for Personal Growth.* New York: New American Library, 1975. Provides comfort while it helps the reader say goodbye to the old relationship and move on.

Rofes / The Fayerweather Street School. *The Kids Book About Divorce: By, For, and About Kids.* Lexington, Mass: The Lewis Publishing Company, 1981. Older children and teenagers express their thoughts and feelings while offering advice and guidance to parents, children, and teens.

◆

Displaced Homeworkers Network, 1411 K Street, NW, Suite 930, Washington, DC 20005; (202) 628-6767. Information, publications, and referrals to one of their nationwide programs for help with emotional and practical issues.

Parents Without Partners 8807 Colesville Road, Silver Spring, MD 20910; (301) 588-9354. Membership and support group for single parents and their children.

We Care, 919 Lanfond Ave., St. Paul, MN 55104; (612) 292-8423. A group for the separated, widowed, and divorced. Trained volunteers, telephone support.

Women on Their Own (W.O.T.O.), Box O, Malaga, NJ 08328; (609) 728-4071. Support, advocacy, networking, and services for working women who are single, divorced, separated, or widowed, and are raising children on their own.

Step Family Association, 28 Allegheny Ave., Suite 1307, Baltimore, MD 21204; (301) 823-7570. A national organization, with state divisions and chapters, that acts as a support network and national advocate for stepparents, remarried parents, and their children. Publishes *Stepfamily Bulletin*.

EATING DISORDERS

Cauwels, J. *Bulimia: The Binge Purge Compulsion*. New York: Doubleday, 1983. What causes and how to alter this destructive pattern.

Orbach, S. *Fat Is a Feminist Issue*. New York: Berkley, 1982. Puts the underlying issues about overeating, dieting, and the preoccupation with appearance in a larger social context.

Roth, G. *Breaking Free from Compulsive Eating*. New York: Bobbs-Merrill, 1984. Focuses on the emotional hungers that lead to overeating.

Siegel, M., J. Brisman, and M. Weinshel. *Surviving an Eating Disorder*. New York: Harper & Row, 1987. Expert and reassuring advice about how to recognize and cope with eating disorders.

◆

Anorexia Nervosa and Associated Eating Disorders (ANAD), Box 271, Highland Park, IL 60035; (312) 831-3438. Provides educational material, reading lists, referrals to support groups and therapists, and assistance in starting support groups that are led by members, with health-care professionals as sponsors.

Overeaters Anonymous, PO Box 90278, Los Angeles, CA 90009; (213) 542-8363. A nationwide program for understanding and overcoming the problems of compulsive overeating.

ETHNIC ISSUES

Grier, W. H., and P. M. Cobbs. *Black Rage*. New York: Basic Books, 1980. Two psychiatrists explore the psychology of blacks—includes a chapter on mental illness and treatment.

McGoldrich, M., J. K. Pearce, and J. Giordano. *Ethnicity and Family Therapy*. New York: Guilford Press, 1982. Papers demonstrating how ethnic factors shape family life and family therapy.

Thomas, A., and S. Sillen. *Racism and Psychiatry*. Secaucus, NJ: Citadel Press, 1974.

Willie, C. V., B. M. Kramer, and B. S. Brown, eds. *Racism and Mental Health: Essays*. Pittsburgh: University of Pittsburgh Press, 1974.

◆

Association of Black Social Workers, 261 West 125th St., New York, NY 10027; (212) 749-0470. Will refer you to a local branch of their organization, where you can get the name of a therapist.

National Association of Black Psychologists, Box 55999, Washington, DC 20040-5999; (202) 722-0808. They have a biographical directory and 28 local affiliates.

American Psychological Association publishes a *Directory of Ethnic Minority Human Resources in Psychology,* issued by the Board of Ethnic Minority Affairs, which lists members who are American Indian / Alaska Native; Asian-American / Pacific Islander; Black / Afro-American; and Hispanic.

National Black Women's Health Project / Self-Help Division, 1237 Gordon Ave., NE, Atlanta, GA 30310; (404) 753-0916. Access to nationwide self-help groups empowering black women by focusing on health issues.

GAY AND LESBIAN ISSUES

Clark, D. *Loving Someone Gay.* New York: Signet, 1977. For gays and loved ones; includes a useful section for helpers like teachers, clergy, police, and therapists.

Borhek, M. V. *Coming Out to Parents: A Two Way Survival Guide for Lesbians and Gay Men and Their Parents.* New York: Pilgrim Press, 1983. Gives practical information, advice, and emotional support; useful case examples.

Hall, M. *The Lavender Couch: A Consumer's Guide to Psychotherapy for Lesbians and Gay Men.* Boston: Alyson Publications (Box 2783, Boston, MA 02208; $7.95), 1985. An excellent resource for choosing and using therapy.

Gonsiorek, J. C., ed. *A Guide to Therapy with Gay and Lesbian Clients.* New York: Harrington Park Press, 1985. Useful information about the special issues confronting gay and lesbian clients in therapy—religious and moral issues, gay and bisexual men in a heterosexual marriage, and the stages of development in the coming-out process.

Most professional organizations have a Gay and Lesbian Caucus; write or call the professional organizations listed above for details. A wide variety of services, self-help groups, and other resources exist for lesbians and gays. To locate resources in your area, contact:

National Gay and Lesbian Crisis Line (800) 221-7044 (M–F, 5 P.M.–10 P.M. EST; Sat., 1–5). If calling from Alaska, Hawaii, or area code 212: (212) 529-1604. Has over 4,000 listings—e.g., groups for gay or lesbian parents, programs for elders who are gay, AIDS counseling.

The National Gay Yellow Pages, a comprehensive guide to gay and lesbian services in the U.S. and Canada. Available from Renaissance House, Box

292, Village Station, New York, NY 10014 ($10, postage paid), or call (212) 674-0120. Information about professional services and counseling groups; updated yearly.

HOLOCAUST SURVIVORS / CHILDREN OF SURVIVORS

Bergmann, M., and M. Gucovy. *Generations of the Holocaust.* New York: Basic Books, 1982. Written by psychoanalysts who studied both Jewish survivor families and children of Nazis, this book presents the ways in which children of Holocaust survivors reenact the sufferings of their parents.

Epstein, G. *Children of the Holocaust.* New York: Bantam, 1979. Written by a daughter of survivors; synthesizes research and tells the stories of several children of survivors.

◆

Second Generation, 350 Fifth Avenue, Suite 3508, New York, NY 10118; (212) 594-8765. A local group, loosely affiliated with a national network of similar groups. Contact for the name of an organization in your area.

ILLNESS, BEREAVEMENT, AND WIDOW(ER)HOOD

Cousins, N. *Anatomy of an Illness as Perceived by a Patient: Reflections on Healing and Regeneration.* New York: Bantam, 1981. By the same author: *The Healing Heart.*

Douglas, P. H., and L. Pinshy, in cooperation with the Columbia University Health Services. *The Essential AIDS Fact Book: What You Need to Know to Protect Yourself, Your Family, All Your Loved Ones.* New York: Pocket Books, 1987.

Kübler-Ross, E. *On Death and Dying.* New York: Macmillan, 1969. The classic on this subject, especially useful for its description of dying as process (don't take the stages too literally). By the same author: *Working It Through.*

Kushner, H. *When Bad Things Happen to Good People.* New York: Avon, 1984. Words of comfort and understanding for times of difficulty.

Mortelli, L., F. Peltz, and W. Messena. *When Someone You Know Has AIDS.* New York: Crown, 1987. A practical guide that would also be useful for a person with AIDS, covering legal, spiritual, financial, and emotional issues.

Ram Dass and P. Gorman. *How Can I Help?* New York: Knopf, 1985. A compassionate guide to how to be with someone who is suffering.

Siegel, B. S. *Love, Medicine, and Miracles.* New York: Harper & Row, 1986. A surgeon looks at how exceptional patients work to heal themselves and makes suggestions about how others can too.

Tetelbaum, J. *The Courage to Grieve: Creative Living, Recovery and Growth Through Grief.* New York: Harper & Row, 1980. In addition to dealing with the immediate process of grieving, this book contains valuable information about how to resolve old, unfinished mourning.

◆

AIDS Hotline, (800) 342-2437. Information and referrals.

THEOS (They Help Each Other Spiritually), 717 Liberty Ave., Pittsburgh, PA 15222; (412) 471-7779. A network of support for widowed men and women. Referral to local affiliate, information.

Widowed Persons Service. A program of the American Association of Retired Persons (see page 251). Offers structured programs to help with the process of bereavement, in over 100 locations around the country.

MENTAL ILLNESS / SERIOUS PSYCHOLOGICAL DISTURBANCES

Johnson, J. *Why Suicide?* Nashville, TN: Oliver-Nesonon, 1987. A look at the factors involved in teen suicide, and what to do to prevent it.

Papolos, D. F., and J. Papolos. *Overcoming Depression.* New York: Harper & Row, 1987. Practical advice and information for depressed persons and their families.

Park, C. C., with L. N. Shapiro. *You Are Not Alone: Understanding and Dealing with Mental Illness.* Boston: Little, Brown, 1976. Although some of the reference material in this book is dated, it remains an excellent book for the families of the mentally ill.

Torrey, E. F. *Surviving Schizophrenia: A Family Affair.* New York: Harper & Row, 1983. A clear, informative, and compassionate guide for the families of schizophrenics with a good resources section and bibliography.

◆

National Alliance for the Mentally Ill, 1901 North Fort Meyer Dr., Suite 500, Arlington, VA 22209; (703) 524-7600. Can give you the names of support groups for families of the mentally ill.

National Depressive and Manic Depressive Association, 222 So. Riverside Plaza, Suite 2812, Chicago, IL 60606; (312) 993-0066 / 0069. Support groups for people who suffer from depression or manic depression.

Suicide, (800) 621-4000 (24 hours). Crisis Hot Line for anyone 18 or under.

PARENTING

Balter, L. *Dr. Balter's Child Sense: Understanding and Handling the Common Problems of Infancy and Early Childhood.* New York: Poseidon, 1985.

Boston Women's Health Collective. *Ourselves and Our Children.* New York: Random House, 1978. An excellent guide to all aspects of child rearing, written by parents with a feminist perspective.

Brusko, M. *Living with Your Teenager.* New York: McGraw-Hill, 1986. Practical information and advice about parenting teens.

Faber, A., and E. Mazlish. *Liberated Parents, Liberated Children.* New York:

Avon, 1974. Complete with vivid examples, this excellent and practical book helps parents communicate with their children. By the same authors: *How to Talk So Kids Will Listen and Listen So Kids Will Talk* and *Siblings Without Rivalry: How to Help Your Children to Live Together So You Can Too.*

Fraiberg, S. *The Magic Years: Understanding and Handling the Problems of Early Childhood.* New York: Scribner, 1959. This beautifully written explanation of a child's experience of the world is a must for new parents.

Turecki, S., and L. Tonner. *The Difficult Child.* New York: Bantam, 1985. Informative, supportive practical advice for anyone with an even slightly difficult child.

◆

Your local YW / YMCA or YW / YMHA often have programs for parents.

The Warm Line, New York University, Washington Square, New York, NY 10003; (212) 998-5369. Telephone counseling for parents.

RELATIONSHIPS / INTIMACY

Bach, G. R., and R. M. Deutsch. *Pairing.* New York: Avon, 1981. How to create intimate relationships.

Bach, G. R., and P. Wyden. *The Intimate Enemy: How to Fight Fair in Love and Marriage.* New York: Avon, 1971. An excellent book about how to resolve differences.

Lerner, H. *The Dance of Anger: A Woman's Guide to Changing Patterns of Intimate Relationships.* New York: Harper & Row, 1986.

Pogrebin, L. C. *Among Friends: Who We Like, Why We Like Them, and What We Do with Them.* New York: McGraw-Hill, 1987.

Satir, V. *Peoplemaking* Palo Alto, CA: Science & Behavior Books, 1972. A readable, informative book by a well-known family therapist about families, communication, and self-esteem.

Scarf, M. *Intimate Partners: Patterns in Love and Marriage.* New York: Random House, 1987. An interesting look at couples at different points in their marriage with an explanation of how relationships form and evolve.

SEXUALITY

Barbach, L. *For Yourself: The Fulfillment of Female Sexuality.* Garden City, NY: Anchor Press, 1975. An outstanding resource for women in exploring and accepting their sexuality.

Carnes, P. J. *Out of the Shadows: Understanding Sexual Addiction.* Minneapolis: CompCare Publications, 1985. Understanding and dealing with issues of sexual addiction.

Hajcak, F., and P. Garwood. *Hidden Bedroom Partners: Needs and Motives That Destroy Sexual Pleasure.* San Diego, CA: Libra Press, 1987. How using sex to fulfill nonsexual needs ultimately reduces sexual pleasure.

With suggestions and homework assignments about how to achieve intimacy.

◆

American Association of Sex Educators, Counselors and Therapists, 11 Dupont Circle, NW, Suite 220, Washington, DC 20005; (202) 462-1171. Members handbook lists certified sex counselors and sex therapists by state.

Sexaholics Anonymous, Box 300, Simi Valley, CA 93062; (818) 704-9854.

Sex Addicts Anonymous, Box 3038, Minneapolis, MN 55403; (612) 339-0217.

CO-S.A. (Co-Dependents of Sex Addicts), Box 14537, Minneapolis, MN 55414; (612) 537-6904.

VIETNAM VETERANS

Addlestone, D., and R. Odell. *The Survival Guide.* New York: Ballantine Books, 1986. How to negotiate the system.

Brandon, H. *Casualties: Death in Viet Nam, Anguish and Survival in America.* New York: St. Martin's Press, 1984.

Terry, W. *Bloods: An Oral History of the Viet Nam War by Black Veterans.* New York: Ballantine, 1985. Twenty black veterans give immediate and gripping descriptions of their experiences.

◆

Viet Nam Veterans of America, 2001 S St., NW, Suite 700, Washington, DC 20009; (202) 332-2700.

YOUR AGING PARENTS

Edenberg, M. A. *Talking with Your Aging Parent.* Boston: Shambhala, 1987. A clear and practical guide to discussing sensitive topics like failing health and financial and legal issues.

Silverstone, B., and H. K. Hyman. *You and Your Aging Parent: The Modern Family's Guide to Emotional, Physical, and Financial Problems.* New York: Pantheon Books, 1982. A guide with a full resource section, checklists for evaluating services, and descriptions of common diseases and symptoms of the elderly.

Stafford, F. *Caring for the Mentally Impaired Elderly: A Family Guide.* New York: Holt, 1986. How to recognize and cope with this difficult situation.

◆ Personal Growth ◆

ASSERTIVENESS TRAINING / SELF-ESTEEM

Alberti, R. E., and M. S. Emmons. *Your Perfect Right: A Guide to Assertive Living.* San Luis Obispo: Impact Publishers (Box 1094, San Luis Obispo, CA), 1986. A revised edition of one of the best step-by-step guides.

Clance, P. R. *The Impostor Phenomenon: When Success Makes You Feel Like a Fake.* New York: Bantam, 1985. How to overcome chronic self-doubt hidden behind a mask of success.

DREAMS

Faraday, A. *The Dream Game.* New York: Harper & Row, 1976. An accessible practical guide to understanding dreams.

Fromm, E. *The Forgotten Language: An Introduction to the Understanding of Dreams, Fairy Tales, and Myths.* New York: Grove Press, 1956. A psychoanalytic perspective on the nature of symbolic language and on the theory and art of dream interpretation.

Freud, S. *The Interpretation of Dreams.* New York: Avon, 1965. The seminal work by the originator of psychoanalysis.

Johnson, R. *Inner Work: Using Dreams and Active Imagination for Personal Growth.* New York: Harper & Row, 1986. An excellent description of the Jungian approach to working with dreams and fantasies.

Ullman, M., and N. Zimmerman. *Working With Dreams: Self-Understanding, Problem Solving, and Enriched Creativity Through Dream Appreciation.* New York: Delacorte, 1979. A useful, detailed guide to understanding your dreams.

KEEPING A JOURNAL

Progoff, I. *At a Journal Workshop: The Basic Text and Guide for Using the "Intensive Journal Process."* New York: Dialogue House, 1975. Guidance in how to use diary feedback techniques to increase self-awareness and personal expansion.

Rainer, T. *The New Diary: How to Use a Journal for Self-Guidance and Expanded Creativity.* Los Angeles: J. P. Tarcher, 1978. A clear, detailed description useful for novices and skilled diarists alike.

LIFE PLANNING

Peck, Scott. *The Road Less Traveled.* New York: Touchstone, 1985. How to grow mentally and spiritually by confronting and overcoming problems. By the same author: *People of the Lie: The Hope for Healing Human Evil.*

Sher, B., with A. Gottlieb. *Wishcraft: How to Get What You Really Want.* New York: Ballantine, 1979.

◆

American Association for Counseling and Development, 5999 Stevenson Ave., Alexandria, VA 22304; (703) 823-9800. Has a listing of members who are trained career counselors. Call or write for this information.

LIFE STAGES

Erikson, E. H. *Childhood and Society.* New York: W. W. Norton, 1985. This classic work on the social significance of childhood includes eight critical stages of psychological and social development from childhood through adulthood. By the same author: *Identity and the Life Cycle.*

Sheehy, Gail. *Passages: Predictable Crises of Adult Life.* New York: E. P. Dutton, 1976. By the same author: *Pathfinders,* an inspiring book describing how ordinary people have overcome obstacles in order to have rewarding middle years.

Vaillant, George E. *Adaptation to Life: How the Brightest Came of Age.* Boston: Little, Brown, 1977. Report of a study that followed a group of Harvard men from their eighteenth birthday until their fiftieth year. Shows how the male life cycle progresses under favorable circumstances.

Viorst, Judith. *Necessary Losses: The Loves, Illusions, Dependencies, and Impossible Expectations That All of Us Have to Give Up in Order to Grow.* New York: Ballantine, 1986. An analytically oriented look at how people develop and mature by integrating losses at each stage of life.

GROWING OLDER

Avery, A. C., with E. Furst and D. D. Hammel. *Successful Aging: A Sourcebook for Older People and Their Families.* New York: Ballantine, 1987. Comprehensive and informative.

Boston Women's Health Collective. *The New Our Bodies, Ourselves.* New York: Simon and Schuster, 1984. By the same authors: *Ourselves, Growing Older: Women Aging with Knowledge and Power.* New York: Simon and Schuster, 1988. Helps women cope with both the cultural prejudice and biological changes that occur in the second half of life.

Carter, J., and R. Carter. *Making the Most of the Rest of Your Life.* New York: Random House, 1987. Practical advice for using the middle and older years to their fullest by our ex-President and First Lady.

Fonda, J., with M. McCarthy. *Woman Coming of Age.* New York: Simon and Schuster, 1984. Advice about exercise, nutrition, and general facts about growing older. Don't be daunted by the pictures of Jane; the information is worthwhile.

◆

American Association of Retired Persons, Program Dept., 1909 K St., NW, Washington, DC 20049; (202) 872-4700. Fast becoming one of the most powerful lobbying organizations in this country, AARP provides a wide and invaluable range of educational and community services.

Grey Panthers, 311 S. Juniper St., Suite 601, Philadelphia, PA 19107; (215) 545-6555. A political action organization, with members of all ages focusing on peace, economic issues, and sexism.

Older Women's League, 730 11 St., NW, Suite 300, Washington, DC 20001;

(202) 783-6686. National organization with local chapters, addressing the concerns of mid-life and older women.

MEDITATION / RELAXATION

Adair, M. *Working Inside Out: Tools for Change.* Berkeley, CA: Wingbow Press, 1984. A rich, complex look at developing an inner consciousness through meditation in a way that can change relationships and have an impact on the larger world as well.

Benson, H., with M. Z. Klipper. *The Relaxation Response.* New York: Avon, 1976. Teaches a simple, straightforward, scientific method of meditation, with a special section on lowering high blood pressure.

Ram Dass. *Journey of Awakening: A Meditator's Guidebook.* New York: Bantam, 1978. In addition to practical advice about how to meditate, this book has an excellent resource section, describing a wide range of groups that teach meditation and retreat facilities where meditation is practiced.

SOCIAL AND POLITICAL ISSUES

Clark, T., and D. T. Jaffe. *Towards a Radical Therapy.* New York: Gordon and Breach, 1973.

Laing, R. D., *The Politics of Experience.* New York: Ballantine, 1967. A challenge to conventional theories of mental illness and alienation.

Porter, K., P. Olsen, and D. Rinzler, eds. *Heal or Die: Psychotherapists Confront the Threat of Nuclear Annihilation.* New York: Psychohistory Press, 1987. A collection of essays describing how psychotherapists deal with nuclear and ecological issues.

Szasz, Thomas S. *The Myth of Mental Illness.* New York: Harper & Row, 1961. How the social and political context define what is seen as mental illness.

PSYCHOTHERAPY RESEARCH

Frank, J. D. *Persuasion and Healing.* Revised Edition. New York: Schocken Books, 1974. Also see Frank, J. D. et al., *Effective Ingredients of Successful Interviews.* These books review and synthesize research on the importance of aspects of the therapeutic relationship such as shared expectations about the process, faith in the therapist's expertise, and optimism regarding the likelihood of a successful outcome.

Luborsky, L. and A. H. Auerbach. "The Therapeutic Relationship in Psychodynamic Psychotherapy: Research Evidence and Its Meaning for Practice." In *Psychiatric Update: American Psychiatric Association Annual Review,* Vol. 4, R. E. Hales and A. J. Frances, eds., Washington, D.C.: American Psychiatric Association, 1985, pp. 550–561. An overview of the growing body of evidence suggesting that a good working relationship between client and therapist is a central factor in the success of therapy.

Schacht, T. E. and H. Strupp, "Evaluation of Psychotherapy." In *Comprehensive Textbook of Psychiatry,* Vol. 2, Edition 4, H. I. Kaplan and B. J. Sadoch, eds., Baltimore, MD: Williams and Wilkins, 1985, pp. 1473–1480. A discussion of the results of current studies on the outcome of psychotherapy.

Strupp, H., S. W. Hadley and R. Gomez-Schwartz. *Psychotherapy for Better or Worse: An Analysis of the Problem of Negative Effects.* New York: Jason Aronson, 1977. A thorough look at situations in which there have been unfavorable outcomes to psychotherapy.

Yalom, I. D. See citation under Group Therapy. Also see I. D. Yalom and M. D. Miles, *Encounter Groups, First Facts.* An analysis of what clients get out of group therapy and what makes therapy successful.

Index

About the Authors

Fredda Bruckner-Gordon, D.S.W., a psychotherapist in private practice for sixteen years, works with individuals, couples, families, and groups. She has taught and supervised graduate students in casework practice and family therapy, and she is currently Director of Stress Reduction Services at Howard M. Bezoza, M.D. & Associates in New York City.

Barbara Kuerer Gangi, C.S.W., is an analytic psychotherapist with twenty-two years' experience. She helped to establish a feminist therapy service and a divorce and remarriage counseling service, and she comanaged the Referral Service for the New York City Society for Clinical Social Work Psychotherapy. She is currently studying short-term, dynamic therapy.

Geraldine Wallman, D.S.W., has been in clinical practice since 1976. Specializing in individual and group therapy, she also supervises other professionals and conducts seminars and workshops of effective cotherapy in groups. She is a Clinical Member of the International Transactional Analysis Association and a student at the Institute for Core Energetics.